Getting Started with VMware Virtual SAN

Build optimal, high-performance, and resilient software-defined storage on VSAN for your vSphere infrastructure

Cedric Rajendran

BIRMINGHAM - MUMBAI

Getting Started with VMware Virtual SAN

First published: May 2015

Production reference: 1260515

Published by Packt Publishing Ltd.
Livery Place
35 Livery Street
Birmingham B3 2PB, UK.

ISBN 978-1-78439-925-2

www.packtpub.com

Credits

Author
Cedric Rajendran

Reviewers
Jason Langer
Julien Mousqueton
Mario Russo
Vikas Shitole
Akmal Khaleeq Waheed

Commissioning Editor
Ashwin Nair

Acquisition Editor
Kevin Colaco

Content Development Editor
Susmita Sabat

Technical Editors
Rikita Poojari
Aman Preet Singh

Copy Editor
Pranjali Chury

Project Coordinator
Milton Dsouza

Proofreaders
Stephen Copestake
Safis Editing

Indexer
Monica Ajmera Mehta

Graphics
Disha Haria
Jason Monteiro

Production Coordinator
Alwin Roy

Cover Work
Alwin Roy

About the Author

Cedric Rajendran is a staff engineer technical support with VMware. He has around 10 years of experience in the IT space, with a wide exposure to datacenter technologies. He holds a master's degree in business administration and has served extensively in the fields of network operations, technical support, and consulting.

His areas of expertise center around the virtualization of server, storage, and networks, and he has an insatiable appetite for studying emerging technologies in the SDDC arena.

A VMware vExpert in 2014 and a virtualization enthusiast in general, he is a regular speaker at VMware events. He holds certifications with VMware and Microsoft and is also a TOGAF-certified enterprise architect.

You can view his blog at http://virtualknightz.com/.

I would like to dedicate this to book to my wife, Ankita, and my daughter, Samantha. All the time spent on writing this book is borrowed from them and is rightfully theirs, I promise to make up for it from now on.

My deepest gratitude goes out to my dear parents, and my siblings, Dominic and Anita, for always being there when I most needed them.

Special thanks to the entire leadership team and colleagues at VMware GSS for their support and encouragement.

Many thanks to the entire Packt team of reviewers and editors for coordinating the whole effort in getting this book published.

Certain things are just not possible without divine intervention, the mysterious hand that leads you through all impediments. This book would not have been possible without that unseen power. I thank God for all the blessings and guidance at the right time and in just the right quantities to keep me going. In gratitude, some of the proceeds from this book will go out to the children at the Gerizim home (http://gerizimhome.com); they need your support too.

About the Reviewers

Jason Langer works as a solutions architect for a VMware partner in the Pacific Northwest, helping customers achieve their datacenter server virtualization and end user computing goals. He has obtained multiple levels of certification both from Microsoft (MCSE/MCSA) and VMware (VCP/VCAP), and brings over 15 years of IT experience to the table. When not working at his day job, Jason is active in the VMware community as a member of the Seattle VMUG Steering Committee and generates content for his blog, http://www.virtuallanger.com/.

He worked as the technical reviewer for *VMware ESXi CookBook* and *Troubleshooting vSphere Storage*, and *VMware Horizon View 5.3 Design Patterns and Best Practices*, all published by Packt Publishing.

Julien Mousqueton has been in the Information Technology field for 16 years, starting out as a systems administrator. Along the way, he worked at different positions, such as an IT manager, a systems engineer, and, most recently, as the chief technology officer (CTO) for a financial group. Currently, he works as a senior consultant in an independent provider of IT infrastructure services.

In addition, Julien is the leader of the French VMware User Group. VMware awarded him a vExpert in 2009.

Mario Russo has worked as an IT architect, a senior technical VMware trainer, and in the pre-sales department. He has been working on the VMware technology since 2004.

In 2005, he worked for IBM on the first large project consolidation for Telecom Italia on the Virtual VMware Esx 2.5.1 platform in Italy with the Physical to Virtual (P2V) tool.

In 2007, he conducted a drafting course and training for BancoPosta, Italy, and project disaster and recovery (DR Open) for IBM and EMC.

In 2008, he worked for the project Speed Up Consolidation BNP and the migration of P2V on VI3 infrastructure at BNP Cardif Insurance.

In 2014, he completed a project on customizing the dashboard and tuning smart alert VCOPs 5.7 for PosteCom, Italy, Rome.

He is a VCI-Certified Instructor 2s Level of VMware and is certified VCAP5-DCA, VCP3-4, VCP5-DVVCP5-DT, and VCP-Cloud.

He is the owner of Business to Virtual, which specializes in virtualization solutions.

He was also the technical reviewer of the following books:, *Implementing VMware Horizon View 5.2, Implementing VMware vCenter Server, Troubleshooting vSphere Storage, VMware Horizon View 5.3 Design Patterns and Best Practices, Instant Getting Started with VMware Fusion, Implementing VMware vCenter Server*, and *VMware vSphere Security Cookbook* all by Packt Publishing.

I would like to thank my wife, Lina, and my daughter, Gaia. They're my strength.

Vikas Shitole is a member of the technical staff at VMware R and D, where he primarily contributes to the vSphere API team, which is focused on vCenter server features such as vSphere DRS, DPM, SDRS, SIOC, and so on. He was awarded vExpert 2014 and 2015, a recognition from VMware for outstanding contributions to the virtualization and cloud computing community. Also, he is the owner of `http://vThinkBeyondVM.com`, a blog site focused on VMware and virtualization. He has completed his M.Tech in computer science from VIT University, India, and holds VCP51, OCPJP 1.6, and MCTS certifications. He can be followed on twitter at `@vThinkBeyondVM`.

Akmal Khaleeq Waheed is a Cloud consultant who specializes in VMware Technologies in all categories. He has previously worked on enterprise servers at Hewlett Packard, and Virtualization at VMware, Inc. He is a VCP (all categories), VCAP (DCA and Design), vExpert 2014 and 2015, and the first ever winner of the reality competition called Virtual Design Master-vDM001 organized by the VMware community.

You can contact Akmal at www.twitter.com/akmal_waheed, or visit his blog at http://vdm-001.blogspot.in.

He has worked as a technical reviewer for VMware vSphere Resource Management Essentials.

www.PacktPub.com

Support files, eBooks, discount offers, and more

For support files and downloads related to your book, please visit www.PacktPub.com.

Did you know that Packt offers eBook versions of every book published, with PDF and ePub files available? You can upgrade to the eBook version at www.PacktPub.com and as a print book customer, you are entitled to a discount on the eBook copy. Get in touch with us at service@packtpub.com for more details.

At www.PacktPub.com, you can also read a collection of free technical articles, sign up for a range of free newsletters and receive exclusive discounts and offers on Packt books and eBooks.

https://www2.packtpub.com/books/subscription/packtlib

Do you need instant solutions to your IT questions? PacktLib is Packt's online digital book library. Here, you can search, access, and read Packt's entire library of books.

Why subscribe?

- Fully searchable across every book published by Packt
- Copy and paste, print, and bookmark content
- On demand and accessible via a web browser

Free access for Packt account holders

If you have an account with Packt at www.PacktPub.com, you can use this to access PacktLib today and view 9 entirely free books. Simply use your login credentials for immediate access.

Instant updates on new Packt books

Get notified! Find out when new books are published by following @PacktEnterprise on Twitter or the *Packt Enterprise* Facebook page.

Table of Contents

Preface   **v**

**Chapter 1: An Introduction to Software-defined Storage
and VSAN**   **1**
  What is a Software-defined Data Center?   **1**
  The significance of Software-defined Storage   **3**
  The storage choices and form factors of Software-defined Storage   **4**
    Traditional storage   4
    Software-based storage   5
    Hyper-converged solutions   5
  An introduction to VMware Virtual SAN   **6**
  Summary   **8**

Chapter 2: Understanding Virtual SAN   **9**
  Why should I use VSAN?   **9**
  What is VSAN?   **10**
    Building blocks of VSAN   13
      Disk groups   14
      VMFS-L   14
      Storage Policy-Based Management   14
  Where do I start? Back to the drawing board   **15**
    Software requirements   15
    Disk boot device   16
      Local storage and boot from SAN   16
      USB and SD card as boot devices   16
    Disk controller   16
    Disk flash devices   18
    Magnetic disks   19
    Network requirements   19

Some simpler options	**20**
Virtual SAN ready nodes	20
EVO: RAIL	20
Summary	**21**
Chapter 3: Workload Profiling and Sizing	**23**
Capacity planning guidelines	**23**
Profiling workloads	24
Virtual SAN sizing utility	26
Virtual SAN shapes and sizes	**28**
Custom built	28
VSAN ready nodes	29
EVO: RAIL	30
VMware guidelines for sizing and assumptions	31
Summary	**32**
Chapter 4: Getting Started with VSAN – Installation and Configuration	**33**
Key concepts	**33**
Disk groups	33
Virtual SAN network	34
Prerequisite checklist	**35**
Installation workflow	**35**
Hardware specifications	**36**
Server node	**37**
Cluster layout	**37**
Network layout	**38**
Setting up a VSAN cluster	**38**
VSAN ready nodes – installation	**43**
Summary	**43**
Chapter 5: Truly Software-defined, Policy-based Management	**45**
Why do we need policies?	**46**
Understanding SPBM	46
VSAN datastore capabilities	48
Accessing the VSAN datastore capabilities	49
Number of disk stripes per object	50
Number of failures to tolerate	51
Flash read cache reservation	53
Force provisioning	54
Object space reservation	55

Under the hood – SBPM   55
  vSphere APIs for Storage Awareness   55
  Managing Virtual SAN storage providers   56
Summary   **56**
Chapter 6: Architecture Overview   **57**
Why such an architecture?   **57**
Anatomy of I/O   **59**
  Write buffer   59
  Destaging data to a magnetic disk   60
  The read cache   61
    The READ I/O workflow   61
Objects, components, and witnesses   **63**
  What is an object?   63
    A swap object   64
    The virtual machine home namespace   65
    Virtual disks and snapshot delta-disks   66
  Components   66
  A witness   67
  Connecting the dots   67
Internal building blocks of VSAN   **68**
  Reliable datagram transport   69
  Cluster monitoring, membership, and directory services   69
  Cluster level object manager   70
  The distributed object manager   70
    The local log structured object manager   70
VSAN and high availability   **71**
  A magnetic disk failure   72
  A flash device failure   73
  A host failure   74
Summary   **74**
Chapter 7: Design Considerations and Guidelines   **75**
Network optimizations   **75**
  Jumbo frames   76
  Speed of the network interface   77
  Network IO control   78
    Isolation, shares, and limits   78
    Quality of Service   81
Storage configuration optimizations   **82**
  A flash device   82

Magnetic disks	83
I/O controllers	83
Cache-to-capacity ratio	83
A scale-out design	**86**
Backing up your VSAN workloads	**87**
Creating a local backup through VDP	87
Creating a local backup to VMFS/NFS through VDP	88
Creating a remote backup through VDP	88
vSphere Replication to protect VSAN	89
Summary	**90**
Chapter 8: Troubleshooting and Monitoring Utilities for Virtual SAN	**91**
Troubleshooting workflow	**92**
Validating the hardware and configuration limit	92
Understanding the software components of VSAN	93
The ESXCLI namespace	93
Ruby vSphere Console	107
VSAN Observer	116
Summary	**121**
Chapter 9: What's New in VSAN 6.0?	**123**
VSAN architecture types	**123**
Hybrid VSAN	125
All-flash VSAN	125
Disk group creation for an all-flash setup	126
Tagging flash capacity devices through ESXCLI	126
Tagging flash capacity devices through Ruby vSphere Client	127
Validation	127
Points to remember with all-flash VSAN	128
The new on-disk format	**128**
Snapshot enhancements	128
The fault domain	**129**
JBOD support	**130**
Serviceability improvements	**130**
LED locators	130
A what-if scenario	131
The rebalance operation	131
Scalability	**132**
Summary	**133**
Index	**135**

Preface

VMware VSAN is a phenomenal concept, technology, solution, and a product—all in one—that has redefined storage provisioning and management in a vSphere-backed infrastructure. The complexities of the traditional SAN have been replaced with simpler, agile, and scalable storage; the key differentiator with VSAN is the fact that complete control of the storage is at the software stack, truly aligning it with the software-defined datacenter vision.

While VSAN has been made simpler, it still needs to be understood and configured appropriately for optimal outcome. With this book, you will be able to understand, deploy, optimize, and monitor a VSAN-backed infrastructure. Based on various use cases and business needs, you will also be able to define appropriate SLAs and ensure compliance through policies.

Besides administration, you will understand what goes on beneath the surface in terms of the architecture and get an explanation of the components that make up VSAN. This helps in closely understanding the limitations of the product and also equips you to analyze and troubleshoot issues that may surface due to anomalies.

This book discusses the first generation of VSAN, as well as its successors, clearly explaining the refinements made in the newer releases to understand the trade-offs with each version.

What this book covers

Chapter 1, *An Introduction to Software-defined Storage and VSAN*, discusses some fundamental aspects of software-defined storage, its evolution, and its role in SDDC. You will also get an overview and basic understanding of VMware Virtual SAN.

Chapter 2, *Understanding Virtual SAN*, discusses Virtual SAN at a high level and builds a basic understanding of how it is put together.

Chapter 3, Workload Profiling and Sizing, talks about the generic guidelines pertaining to sizing and profiling of Virtual Machines.

Chapter 4, Getting Started with VSAN – Installation and Configuration, demonstrates deploying a simple set up to show the workflow of a typical VSAN deployment.

Chapter 5, Truly Software-defined, Policy-based Management, discusses one of the unique differentiators of Virtual SAN called Storage Policy-Based Management (SPBM).

Chapter 6, Architecture Overview, explains why VSAN has a relatively complex architecture and then discusses the structure and components of VSAN.

Chapter 7, Design Considerations and Guidelines, talks about some of the design considerations and best practices to fine-tune the configuration and ensures optimal performance and availability.

Chapter 8, Troubleshooting and Monitoring Utilities for Virtual SAN, provides a configuration overview, and helps you in assuring the health of the infrastructure and proactively monitoring key metrics and potential issues.

Chapter 9, What's New in VSAN 6.0?, assesses the newer features, enhancements, and architectural changes with the second generation of VSAN.

What you need for this book

For this book, you will require the following software components:

Generation	VSAN Version	vSphere version
Generation 1	VSAN 5.5	ESXi 5.5 Update 1 and Update 2 vCenter 5.5 Update 1 and Update 2
Generation 2	VSAN 6.0	ESXi 6.0 and vCenter 6.0

Who this book is for

This book is intended primarily for virtualization administrators who are keen to learn and understand VMware VSAN and also to help storage administrators to familiarize and adapt to software-defined storage.

Conventions

In this book, you will find a number of styles of text that distinguish between different kinds of information. Here are some examples of these styles, and an explanation of their meaning.

Code words in text, database table names, folder names, filenames, file extensions, pathnames, dummy URLs, user input, and Twitter handles are shown as follows: "The attribute that confirms that the flash device has been tagged successfully is IsCapacityFlash."

Any command-line input or output is written as follows:

```
# vdq -q -d naa.5000c5006bc235b3
\{
"Name"              :  "naa.5000c5006bc235b3",
"VSANUUID           :  "",
"State"             :  "Eligible for use by VSAN",
"ChecksumSupport"   :  "0",
"Reason"            :  "None",
"IsSSD"             :  "1",
"IsCapacityFlash"   :  "1",
"IsPDL"             :  "0",
    \},
```

New terms and **important words** are shown in bold. Words that you see on the screen, in menus or dialog boxes for example, appear in the text like this: "This can be done automatically by setting the VSAN cluster to the **Automatic** mode, as explained in the preceding example".

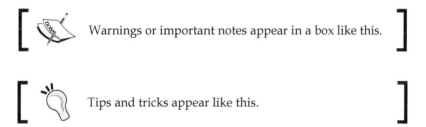

[Warnings or important notes appear in a box like this.   ]

[Tips and tricks appear like this.   ]

Reader feedback

Feedback from our readers is always welcome. Let us know what you think about this book—what you liked or may have disliked. Reader feedback is important for us to develop titles that you really get the most out of.

To send us general feedback, simply send an e-mail to feedback@packtpub.com, and mention the book title via the subject of your message.

If there is a topic that you have expertise in and you are interested in either writing or contributing to a book, see our author guide on www.packtpub.com/authors.

Customer support

Now that you are the proud owner of a Packt book, we have a number of things to help you to get the most from your purchase.

Downloading the example code

You can download the example code files for all Packt books you have purchased from your account at http://www.packtpub.com. If you purchased this book elsewhere, you can visit http://www.packtpub.com/support and register to have the files e-mailed directly to you.

Errata

Although we have taken every care to ensure the accuracy of our content, mistakes do happen. If you find a mistake in one of our books—maybe a mistake in the text or the code—we would be grateful if you would report this to us. By doing so, you can save other readers from frustration and help us improve subsequent versions of this book. If you find any errata, please report them by visiting http://www.packtpub.com/submit-errata, selecting your book, clicking on the **erratasubmissionform** link, and entering the details of your errata. Once your errata are verified, your submission will be accepted and the errata will be uploaded on our website, or added to any list of existing errata, under the Errata section of that title. Any existing errata can be viewed by selecting your title from http://www.packtpub.com/support.

Piracy

Piracy of copyright material on the Internet is an ongoing problem across all media. At Packt, we take the protection of our copyright and licenses very seriously. If you come across any illegal copies of our works, in any form, on the Internet, please provide us with the location address or website name immediately so that we can pursue a remedy.

Please contact us at `copyright@packtpub.com` with a link to the suspected pirated material.

We appreciate your help in protecting our authors, and our ability to bring you valuable content.

Questions

You can contact us at `questions@packtpub.com` if you are having a problem with any aspect of the book, and we will do our best to address it.

1
An Introduction to Software-defined Storage and VSAN

In this chapter, you will learn some fundamental aspects of Software-defined Storage, its evolution, and its role in a Software-defined Data Center. You will also get an overview and a basic understanding of VMware Virtual SAN.

To understand the transformation that is taking place in modern data center, we will discuss:

- What is a Software-defined Data Center?
- The significance of Software-defined Storage
- Storage choices
- An introduction to VMware Virtual SAN

What is a Software-defined Data Center?

Virtualization has come a long way in terms of evolution and dates back to 1960, where mainframes first supported virtualization.

Decades later, leading into the x86 era, there was a strong need to leverage the virtualization concept on a x86 platform. The need was straight and simple, a transition from an application/operating system per server to running multiple such instances per server. The reasons were obvious as well, server hardware capabilities had increased exponentially and much of the server resources were wasted. There was room for the consolidation and optimization of resources, and needless to say, this also meant significant return on investment.

While there were a few players who threw their hats into the ring, not many made a mark. In the year 1998, however, VMware was established and their first product, **Workstation,** made it possible to successfully virtualize the x86 platform. They were also the first to successfully boot Microsoft Windows as a virtual machine. They continue to lead the pack and are the undisputed leaders of this domain. To further endorse this, Gartner named VMware the leader in the Magic Quadrant for x86 server virtualization infrastructure for the fifth consecutive year.

Virtualization starts out creating an abstraction layer on hardware, and then carving out resources and pooling these resources to achieve agility in availability and load balancing. Furthermore, to increase efficiency, we automate tasks.

While virtualization made it very easy to deploy workloads from a computing perspective, there were still organizational silos and the inevitable dependencies on storage requirements and network requirements to complete the provisioning. Hence the concepts of abstraction, pooling, and automation, which made compute virtualization simplified, extended to storage and network as well. This paved the way to the concept of the **Software-Defined Data Center (SDDC)**, as shown in the following figure:

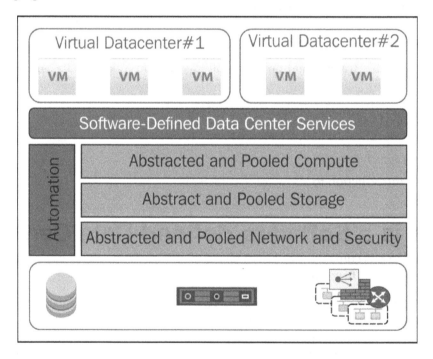

To understand SDDC, we must start by clarifying that it is not a data center controlled merely by automation or scripting. As depicted in the previous figure, it is rather the creation of abstraction layers for compute, storage, network, and security that are managed at the software layer on top of which virtual data centers are built and scaled.

Thus, the three key pillars of SDDC are:

- Computing/server virtualization
- Software-Defined Storage
- Software-Defined Networking

The former CTO of VMware, Steve Herrod, describes SDDC as:

> *"Software-defined means (1) abstract logical from physical (2) distribute functionality (3) manage as single system."*

In this book, we will discuss Software-Defined Storage and VMware's flagship product in this area—VMware Virtual SAN.

The significance of Software-defined Storage

Traditionally, storage was confined to the server's hardware; eventually, due to the increasing demand for storage capacity, availability, and centralized management, there was a need for a robust system to manage storage provisioning and maintenance. This lead to the evolution of **storage area network** (**SAN**) and **Network Attached Storage** (**NAS**). While a typical Fiber Channel, SAN, proved to be quite expensive, particularly the Fabric switch and the array itself, it also had other form factors that leveraged the existing network infrastructure in the form of iSCSI and NFS. Interestingly, a complete cycle of evolution is taking place and we are heading back toward storage being confined to the server and forming one of the methodologies of achieving Software-Defined Storage.

In a typical data center, we have several types of resource-intensive workloads that can be compute-, network-, memory-, or disk- intensive. While the compute and network needs are serviced by server virtualization solutions, such as ESXi, and network virtualization solutions, such as NSX, all the workloads need disk capacity, but with varying requirements in terms of redundancy and performance. The storage resources need to be elastic and dynamic, catering to different I/O requirements.

This implied that we needed a much more granular and dynamic management of the storage infrastructure, and such a degree of control can only be achieved at the software stack; we needed Software-Defined Storage.

Very simply put, Software-Defined Storage can be defined as a storage infrastructure that can be fully managed at the software stack.

Software-Defined Storage is truly aligned with the SDDC vision of the abstraction, pooling and automation of all the data center's resources.

The deliverable of Software-Defined Storage is a Virtual Data Service that is policy - driven; the three primary attributes of this deliverable are:

- Performance
- Data protection
- Mobility

While the SDS market is densely populated with various different players, the market is highly disruptive and evolving heavily, we will look at a few form factors available as on date.

The storage choices and form factors of Software-defined Storage

To better understand the value proposition of SDS, one should understand the current state of affairs, options at disposable, and the advantages of each option leading to the newest fad in enterprise storage; in this section, we will closely evaluate these options.

Traditional storage

Storage arrays, such as EMC-Clariion and HP EVA/MSA, are some examples of traditional storage. These are presented in their raw form, and their conventional storage management software comes along with them, most often lacking intelligence, unaware of the consumers and workloads albeit at a high level. For instance, we define the host mode as Windows/Unix indicating that the server accessing the array has a specific type of operating system, such that any known optimizations for the OS can be applied. This, of course, does not suffice the level of intelligence that can enable Software-Defined Storage. Nonetheless, the traditional storage may continue to exist for several unique reasons and certain advantages/ features until Software-Defined Storage is completely adapted. Most likely, these will eventually shape up as commodity hardware and the offload management capability to the software stack, and then these will converge to SDS; until such time, this technology will complement SDS.

Software-based storage

Innovating from traditional storage solutions, software-based storage solutions decouple the basic management capabilities (if existent) or take commodity hardware and govern it through the software stack. Microsoft Windows Server storage space and Red Hat Gluster are some examples of software-based storage solutions. What is being sold here is purely software, and the choice of hardware is slightly flexible and commonly outlined in a compatibility list. The key thing to note is that the software only manages the storage and is not combined with the compute/server virtualization platform.

Hyper-converged solutions

As the name indicates, Hyper-converged solutions unify the compute, storage and/or network under one roof. That is, one or more vendors will provide a packaged solution that will come in the form of a set of hardware that provides storage and network capabilities with a choice of hypervisors such as VMware ESXi or Microsoft Hyper-V.

In summary, Hyper-converged solutions arguably pose as hybrid solutions stemming out off and, effectively, may replace traditional SAN and Software-based Storage.

Of particular importance in this area and a key differentiator among the rest, is the VMware VSAN solution, wherein an abstraction layer for storage is in-built in the hypervisor. VMware has cranked up a notch ahead on this note and carved out a significant milestone with EVO: RAIL, an evolutionary Hyper-Converged Infrastructure Appliance (HCIA). This is done in partnership with an elite list of hardware vendors, in essence, vSphere and Virtual SAN are sold and supported in a box.

So what's the big difference?

* VSAN natively understands vSphere Storage needs — this is crucial in terms of performance
* Other Hyper-converged vendors need a controller VM to provide the storage abstraction, while for VSAN, this becomes a feature to be enabled
* With some basic configuration settings after racking and stacking, you are ready to deploy the VMs
* There is a single point of support for all issues

- There is no specialized skill set needed to be a vSphere administrator than a bit of reading from this book!!!

- In particular, EVO: RAIL is an all-inclusive licensing model, shipping with vSphere Enterprise Plus 5.5 U2 and includes the licenses needed for vCenter, ESX, VMware VSAN, and LogInsight

EVO: RAIL carves out an SDDC with these simple steps:

1. Procuring the appliance, racking and stacking it
2. Connecting to the top of the rack switch
3. Attaching your laptop to the switch and connecting to the RAIL IP address

If you are in a real hurry, just click on "Just Go!" and you are all set to deploy Virtual Machines.

Here is a sneak peek at the configuration screen of EVO: RAIL:

An introduction to VMware Virtual SAN

Here is the definition provided by VMware — "VMware Virtual SAN is a new software-defined storage tier for VMware vSphere environments. Virtual SAN clusters server disks and flash to create radically simple, high - performance, resilient shared storage designed for virtual machines."

They say history repeats itself; true to this, we have completed a cycle moving from server-based in-built storage to storage array networks (SAN), we did this primarily for the following two basic key requirements:

- **Scalability**: The local disk capacity was insufficient
- **Mobility and Resiliency**: Server-based disks proved to be a single point of failure

Hence, moving to SAN storage addressed these requirements and brought to the table many more advantages, it also brought a challenge along in terms of cost.

The cost factor was, by itself, a significant driver to move away from the SAN infrastructure back into server-based storage.

VMware Virtual SAN is one such solution (arguably the best) that eliminates the limitations of server-based storage and optimizes performance by coupling hard disks with flash storage in its first generation. With the latest release, VSAN 6.0 supports all flash storage.

At a high level, the following diagram depicts a four node cluster that provides HDDs and SSDs formulating a Virtual SAN Clustered Datastore which, in turn, serves as the abstraction layer on which vSphere platform provides the disk capabilities for the Virtual Machine deployment.

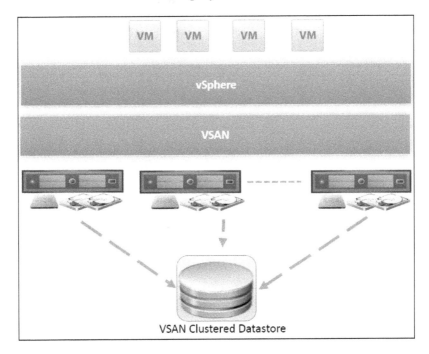

Furthermore, we can implement granular control to frame individual virtual machine-level policies. Through policies, we can govern service-level agreements and the requirements of the workloads.

At the very root, while designing a virtual machine, the requirements are driven by the operating system and the application that will be contained in the virtual machine, that is, the requirements in terms of CPU, memory, disk, and network. All of the resources need to work in tandem to ensure that the end user experience meets the expectations/service-level agreements. From a disk perspective, the business will be interested in IOPS and redundancy, these requirements are embedded in virtual machine storage policies that will ensure that a virtual machine obtains the entitled resources during its lifecycle.

Summary

The future of IT is inclined toward a Software-defined Datacenter, whether it is on-premises or off-premises. Software-defined storage is the factor that accelerates this adaption by providing a very high degree of control and dynamism to Storage Management and Provisioning. While the directive is clear, the means of achieving software-define storage are aplenty. The question is, which solution will be optimal and be more advantageous than the rest? There are very strong indicators that a hybrid model that is cost-effective will lead the way, VMware have their noses ahead with Virtual SAN & EVO: RAIL. We have discussed the options available thus far and will closely assess the nitty-gritty aspects of VMware Virtual SAN in the upcoming chapters.

2
Understanding Virtual SAN

In the first chapter, we discussed in detail SDDC, the role of software-defined storage, the current choices of storage in the market, and also an introduction to VMware Virtual SAN. In this chapter, we will turn our focus to what Virtual SAN is and build a basic understanding of how it is put together.

The following topics will be discussed in this chapter:

- Why should I use VSAN
- What is VSAN
- Where do I start? Back to the drawing board

Why should I use VSAN?

In this section, we'll discuss about the advantages of leveraging VSAN and its key differentiators.

Imagine a large environment with a heterogeneous cluster of storage provisioned from different arrays through iSCSI/FC/NFS. An administrator has to be skilled and knowledgeable in building and maintaining all of the components or, as in most cases, will have to depend on storage, network administrators, and various other teams and vendors to build and maintain such a setup.

Furthermore, beyond building and maintaining such a setup, the excruciating aspect would be when something breaks down in the environment, a true "needle in a haystack" situation. The complexity results in prolonged outages and multivendor coordination, and the root cause can be anything between an administrator tripping a cable and a software or hardware defect.

Now, compare this with only needing to worry about a set of hyper-converged x86 servers, just like the old just like old times, to build standalone servers', you can simply rack, stack and install the OS.

The VSAN solution makes this possible by integrating with vSphere without the need to install additional VIBs, and takes out the bells and whistles of a traditional SAN.

Performance is optimized through two key mechanisms — read caching and write buffering. In essence, almost every I/O is processed through flash and so, a greater degree of performance is achieved. This is of course, apart from leveraging the traditional RAID concepts as well, to increase availability and performance.

Furthermore, scalability with VSAN simply implies that you append storage capacity to the physical hardware (up to the maximum capacity supported by the specific hardware) or just add more servers to the VSAN cluster to augment compute/storage.

VSAN can support, co-exist and interoperate with key features such as vMotion, Storage vMotion, Virtual Machine Snapshots, HA & DRS to name a few. In short, we have all the advantages of hosting virtual machine data on traditional SAN and, in addition, we have granular control.

What is VSAN?

Let's start with a simple comparison: Virtual SAN is to storage as vSphere is to compute. In other words, VSAN revolutionizes storage in a very similar way to how vSphere or virtualization, in general, revolutionized x86 servers.

VSAN has evolved through two generations so far, the first generation embedded with the vSphere 5.5.x stream (update 1 and higher) and the second generation commenced with vSphere 6.0. In this section, we will discuss the first generation to keep things simple and cover the newer features, enhancements, and architectural changes in the second generation of VSAN in *Chapter 9, What's New in VSAN 6.0?*.

The key features of VSAN are as follows:

- Use a combination of **solid state disk (SSD)** or PCIe flash devices with HDD (magnetic disks) to provide a server-based storage solution
- SSD is leveraged to optimize performance
- HDD provides the capacity

All read and write I/O will be funneled through the flash device, which will act as the first point reference. In most cases, a flash device suffices to service the I/O, while in certain circumstances, there could be reads that need to be serviced from the magnetic disks. The percentage of flash disk to magnetic disk is recommended to be approximately 10 percent. This model helps serve the fundamental concept of VSAN, wherein a magnetic disk is used as the persistent store for the data and flash devices are used as an acceleration layer.

At a very high level, the following illustration reflects what we strive to achieve:

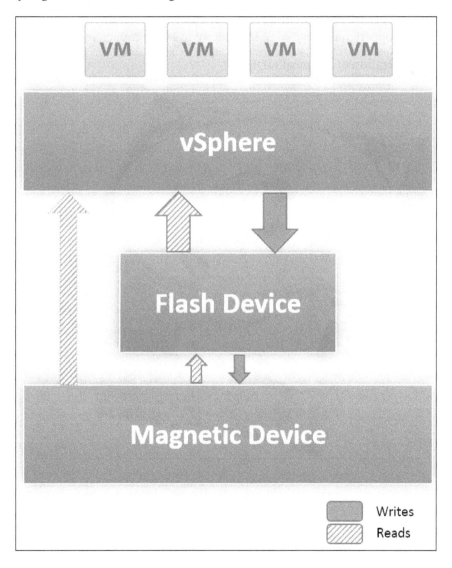

A flash device or solid state disk is an electronic disk; ironically, there is no real "disk" that spins. The data is persistently stored through integrated circuit assemblies. The interfaces to SSD are still compatible traditional block I/O disk drives, which make it easier to replace/swap/interchange HDDs with SSDs.

SSDs have no moving parts. This clearly draws the line between the mechanical and magnetic HDDs that work through spindles, platters, and magnetic heads on an actuator arm to read and write data. This also makes the SSDs much more superior in terms of performance with very less latency.

While the cost of SSD continues to be exponentially higher than conventional HDDs, we leverage proportional usage of SSD capacity to HDD capacity.

Here is an illustration of a typical HDD:

Here is an illustration of an SSD:

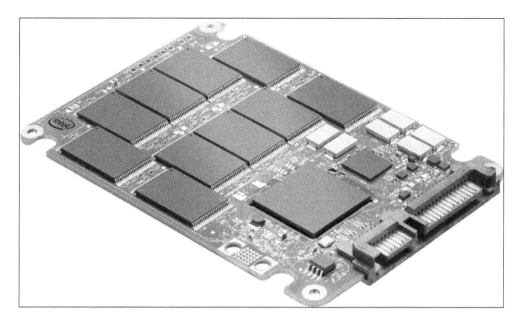

Building blocks of VSAN

Virtual SAN stores and manages data in the form of flexible data containers called objects. An object is a logical volume that has its data and metadata distributed and accessed across the entire cluster, which is very different from how VMware's hypervisor stored and managed data traditionally. Hence, with VSAN, there was a clear requirement to redefine the conventional VMFS layout. This gave birth to the VMFS-L filesystem, diskgroup concept and overall created a paradigm shift from storing files to storing objects. Furthermore, there was a need for a software-defined mechanism to apply and maintain certain governance to the objects stored. This is achieved through SPBM.

In this section, we will examine the VSAN structure and layout by understanding the role of:

- Disk groups
- VMFS-L, which is a derived file system
- Storage Policy Based Management

Disk groups

Disk groups are management constructs carved out with a combination of SSD and HDD. On each host that contributes storage, the available disks are claimed, pooled, and organized into one or more disk groups; these disk groups form the main unit of storage on a host. These units cumulatively form the VSAN datastore in the cluster.

A disk group layout should adhere to the following outlined limitations:

Artifacts	Minimums	Maximums
Disk Groups	One per host	Five per host
Flash devices like SAS, SATA, PCIe SSD	One per disk group	One per disk group
Magnetic disk devices	One HDD per disk group	Seven HDDs per disk group
Disk formatting overhead	750 MB per HDD	750 MB per HDD

The formation of disk groups based on the outlined limitations sets the platform to carve out the VMFS-L filesystem.

VMFS-L

Conventionally, the **Virtual Machine File System** (**VMFS**) was designed and optimized for clustering purposes. This is reasonable, since multiple hosts seek access to perform metadata modifications, while a variety of I/O were read and written to the data region concurrently. For Virtual SAN, the requirements were subtly different such as the locality of the devices and the non-requirement of certain clustering features. Due to this unique nature, a modified object-based derivative was formulated called **VMFS-Local** (**VMFS-L**). This modified file system specifically aids in an object-oriented approach by providing storage services.

Storage Policy-based Management

Finally, to align with the software-defined storage vision, **Storage Policy Based Management** (**SPBM**) helps define the actual policies associated to each object that is stored in a VSAN datastore. There are five key attributes for each object, which dictate the availability and performance of the specific object.

To connect the dots, we perform the following steps:

1. We start by organizing the physical disks to form disk groups on each ESXi host.
2. Create a VSAN datastore by pooling the various disk groups from hosts in the cluster.
3. Create policies that govern how each object is stored in the VSAN datastore.

We will discuss the concept of objects in greater detail in *Chapter 6, Architecture Overview*.

Where do I start? Back to the drawing board

We can get started with VSAN by following a traditional practice to get your feet wet in lab/test (dev set up is recommended for this).

Furthermore, it is important to ensure that, for any solution, the components need to be certified and should be listed in the compatibility matrices of VMware.

VSAN, in particular, is sensitive to this and comes in a few variants or packages. You can either choose to select the components individually and assemble, or choose a much safer option and go for a bundled solution.

Software requirements

At the time of writing, the supported releases to build a VSAN are as follows:

vSphere components	Versions supported	Specifications(per host)
ESXi version	vSphere ESXi 5.5 update 1 (and higher)	6 GB memory At least 1 SDD At least 1 HDD
vCenter versions	vCenter Server 5.5 update 1 (and higher) vCenter Server Appliance 5.5 update 1 (and higher)	Follow the standard sizing guidelines

The VSAN cluster enables a dynamic scale out model; you can either choose to scale with compute resources, or storage resources, or both. Beyond the initial three hosts, it is not a mandate that all hosts contribute storage and they can simply serve as a compute only node.

Disk boot device

While using the VSAN, the ESXi host can be booted from USB device, SD card, local storage, or SAN LUN.

There are, however, certain limitations with some boot devices. One significant factor influencing the boot device is the VSAN trace. Tracing comprises of the information about the I/O transaction that aids in troubleshooting and in general is sought by VMware technical support and engineering for diagnosing certain issues.

Local storage and boot from SAN

Local storage or a boot from SAN are supported as boot devices similar to any standard vSphere ESXi deployment.

USB and SD card as boot devices

USB and SD cards are supported as boot devices as long as the physical memory on the server hardware does not exceed 512 GB.

The minimum size for the USB or SD card device must be 4GB.

The rationale behind this caveat of USB/SD not being supported with servers with memory larger than 512 GB is that, apart from storing the core dumps when there is a crash, the VSAN traces are also written to the USB device. Hence, there is a possibility that the core dump partition may not be sufficient to hold memory dumps as well as VSAN traces.

Note that the Virtual SAN trace file RAMDisk size should not be increased over the default 300 MB size.

Disk controller

Controllers can operate in either of the two modes outlined here:

- Pass through mode
- RAID 0 mode

Ensure that the controller supports at least one of these two modes.

The pass through mode allows the hypervisor to have greater control over the underlying drives, so that the performance, capacity, and redundancy is managed by VSAN.

Alternatively, the RAID 0 mode allows the creation of a single-drive RAID 0 through the storage controller software utilizing all SSDs and HDDs within the Virtual SAN cluster.

The single-drive RAID 0 set is then presented to Virtual SAN. To distinguish SSD from HDD, ESXCLI namespaces are used explicitly to mark the specific device as SSD.

Note that SSD detection should be automatic. However, RAID configuration or other controller issues may require explicit declaration.

The following are the controller feature names/types listed in the VMware compatibility guide along with their corresponding support for Virtual SAN in pass through or RAID 0 mode:

Component	Mode
Virtual SAN SAS	IT mode controller, supports pass-through
Virtual SAN SATA	IT mode controller, supports pass-through
Virtual SAN RAID 0	RAID controller, supports RAID 0 mode
Virtual SAN pass through	RAID controller, supports pass through (JBOD mode)

IT mode refers to initiator target mode, a commonly used term in storage controller HBAs, whereas in RAID the similar concept is referenced as JBOD.

One critical aspect of choosing the appropriate controller is the queue depth: the minimum required queue depth is 256 however, the higher, the better. This is because the controller queue depth risks posing a bottleneck with multiple workloads/virtual machines generating I/O, all funneled through the controller. Given its significance, the VSAN hardware compatibility list includes this as one of the key parameters while you attempt to validate. This is depicted in the following screenshot:

Brand Name	Model	Feature	Product Description	Queue Depth	Supported Releases
Cisco	UCS-RAID9271CV-8I	Virtual SAN RAID 0	Device Type: SAS-RAID VID: 1000 SVID: 1000 DID: 005B SSID: 9271	1024	ESXi 5.5 U2 ESXi 5.5 U1
DELL	Dell PERC H200 Adapter	Virtual SAN Pass-Through	Device Type: SAS/SATA-RAID VID: 1000 SVID: 1028 DID: 0072 SSID: 1F1D	600	ESXi 5.5 U2 ESXi 5.5 U1

Disk flash devices

Flash devices are the most crucial components that will help increase the performance. SAS, SATA, and PCIe devices are the supported interfaces for flash devices.

Flash devices are categorized based on the write performance and the choice of hardware can be filtered to cater to the requirements:

Classes	Writes per second
Class A	2500 to 5000
Class B	5000 to 10000
Class C	10000 to 20000
Class D	20000 to 30000
Class E	30000 and more

Aside from the write metrics, the endurance of a flash device is also validated by the number of **Diskful Writes Per Day** (**DWPD**) that can be performed over the lifetime of the device. The higher the DWPD value, the better the reliability.

Detailed information of components and their compatibility with VSAN can be found at `http://www.vmware.com/resources/compatibility/search.php?deviceCategory=vsan`.

Here is a screenshot of what you can expect to see:

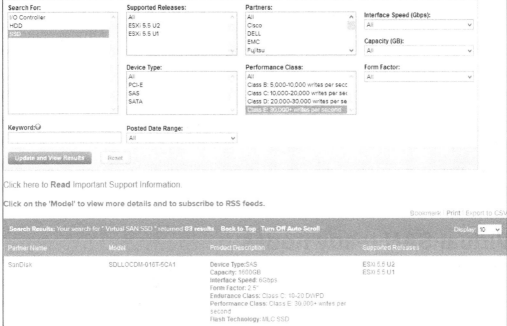

Magnetic disks

Magnetic disks provide the actual storage capacity for the VSAN datastore. Magnetic disk are categorized based on RPM of 7200, 10000, and 15000. VMware recommends 7200 RPM drives for capacity, and 10000 RPM and 15000 RPM drives for performance; 10000 RPM drives are cost effective.

Network requirements

VSAN requires a minimum of 1 GbE NIC to be configured as a VSAN VMkernel port. The port is used for intercluster node communication and also for reading/writing to objects external to the ESXi host. This network needs to be dedicated to the VSAN traffic.

Although the minimum requirement is 1 GbE NIC, it is highly recommended to have a 10 GbE NIC for better throughput. Furthermore, with a 10 GbE NIC, the port can be used to carry other non-VSAN traffic, provided that the bandwidth is guaranteed through vSphere network I/O control, a vSphere VDS feature.

VSAN also requires multicast to be enabled in the layer two network. This facilitates the internode communication.

Although not mandatory, network redundancy, enabling jumbo frames, and leveraging vSphere network IO control provide better resiliency and throughput; these will be discussed in *Chapter 7, Design Considerations and Guidelines*.

Some simpler options

If manually assembling the components is found to be cumbersome, there are two simpler options:

- Virtual SAN ready nodes
- EVO: RAIL

Virtual SAN ready nodes

Virtual SAN ready nodes are hyper-converged nodes that are sold by server OEMs. These readymade nodes are generally preconfigured to run vSphere with VSAN that have been tested/certified, and come in a specialized and optimized hardware form factor.

Virtual SAN ready nodes also provide a detail of combination of hardware resources in terms of the size, type, and quantity of the CPU, memory, network, I/O controller, HDD, and SSD, combined with a certified server that is best suited to run a specific Virtual SAN workload.

Furthermore, the OEM vendors provide a sizing classification with low, medium, and high profiles for server workloads, and full clone and linked clone profiles for VDI workloads. These can be used as guidance to design and deploy solutions catering to business needs.

EVO: RAIL

EVO: RAIL is the complete package, a **Hyper-Converged Infrastructure Appliance (HCIA)**. It comes in a single SKU with a highly simplified configuration engine requiring very minimal user intervention.

A single EVO: RAIL appliance comprises of four servers/nodes and can be scaled out to a total of four appliances (or 16 ESXi hosts/nodes).

Outlined here are the specifications of a single appliance:

- 48 CPU cores
- 768 GB memory capacity
- 14.4 TB storage capacity
- 1.6 TB flash capacity
- 80 GbE network bandwidth

EVO: RAIL is an easy choice when it comes to building a VSAN-backed infrastructure.

Summary

We established why a solution such as VSAN can simplify the administration of IT in terms of skill and cost and yet provide better performance and availability.

We also gained a basic understanding of VSAN and the components that make up the architecture. Furthermore, we built a step-by-step definition of the minor details and importance of each component; this is of particular significance if one intends to assemble VSAN. We delved into some simpler options that ease the sophistication of verifying each and every component by choosing a VSAN ready node and the next-gen form factor of VSAN through EVO: RAIL.

When we move on to the next chapter, there will be more emphasis on specific examples, profiling, and sizing based on the workloads.

3
Workload Profiling and Sizing

So far, we have built a good understanding of VSAN and its types at a high level. Progressing in this chapter, we will discuss generic guidelines pertaining to sizing and profiling of virtual machines.

The guidelines are generalized based on their use, whether they are desktops or servers. The focus of this chapter is on getting the right VSAN composition and capacity based on the workload requirements.

We will discuss the following objectives:

- Capacity planning
- Types of VSAN and their uniqueness
- Adaption of sizing guidelines on different types of VSAN

Capacity planning guidelines

Capacity planning has been made easy while designing a VSAN-backed cluster. Conceptually, the scale-out model helps in augmentation of resources and to strike the right balance between compute and storage, that is, you can choose to add either storage or disk based on which resource you are running out of or exhausting. Such design aids in ensuring that the environment is neither oversized nor undersized.

Most importantly, having a flexible architecture accommodates the ad hoc nature and elasticity that is synonymous with a software-defined data center.

We will work through the process of identifying the types of virtual machines that typically exist in today's IT organizations and how we can fit them in a VSAN-backed cluster.

Profiling workloads

Each workload is unique and has varying requirements. However, we can generalize workloads for the ease of sizing, estimation, and capacity planning. Let's take an example of what typically exists in our data centers. We are likely to have users' desktops (with Windows XP or Windows 8 operating system) that are hosted on the vSphere platform or servers that provide mail services, database services, or run similar services/applications. Thus, classification of workloads can primarily be based on VDI and server workloads. These are further subclassified as follows:

- Virtual desktop infrastructure
  - Linked clones
  - Full clones
- Server profiles
  - High
  - Medium
  - Low

For a VDI-backed infrastructure, the VM can either be a linked or full clone; the differentiator is that, for a full clone, the required storage capacity is almost exponential. For server profiles, the differentiator is the consolidation ratio, that is, the number of VM's per host.

While this classification is most appropriate for a VDI-backed infrastructure, in the sense that most organizations have standardized images (desktop OS, word processing applications, mail client, and so on), this would be provided to their employees. From a pure operations perspective, you are likely to have templates for each department with very minor customizations allowed for the end user to perform. So, generalizing is safe.

On the other hand, for server profiles, there are several permutations and combinations of resource requirements. To generalize, server profile can either be predictive or adaptive. A server profile is predictive when we know the applications' virtual hardware requirement and it is adaptive where we size based on assumptions or estimations and tweak based on utilization.

It is prudent to take a pragmatic approach as generic guidelines, while designing server class workloads, can take off into a different tangent. We trust in the law of averages and need to consider minor tweaking based on the nature of the application.

The key factors influencing workload profiles are as follows:

- **Consolidation ratio**: This will decide the number of workloads or virtual machines you intend to deploy per host depending on the type of workload. The choice of server hardware specification will vary, that is, fewer high-end servers versus several low-end servers, or a balance between the two.

- **IOPS ratio**: This is the ratio of reads versus writes expected; this significantly varies between a desktop and a server virtual machine. A desktop workload is expected to be 30 percent reads and 70 percent writes. For a server profile, the roles are reversed with 70 percent IO being reads. This plays a key consideration in the SSD to HDD ratio.

- **SSD to HDD ratio**: This is the ratio of flash device to magnetic device. Note that this is prior to the consideration of the number of failures to tolerate. More details on this are discussed in *Chapter 5, Truly Software-defined, Policy-based Management*. VMware recommends to have flash size targeted at 10 percent of the anticipated consumed space. This, in turn, governs the size of the flash devices and magnetic devices, in other words, the composition of the disk group. A maximum of seven disks are permitted in a disk group and each disk group can have a maximum of one SSD.

As you can imagine, for the same number of virtual machines you intend to put on a node, the size of the flash should be much higher for full clones (entire VM) as opposed to linked clones (shared disks).

VMware has provided estimated hardware requirements for the various workload profiles at `http://partnerweb.vmware.com/programs/vsan/Virtual%20SAN%20 Hardware%20Quick%20Start%20Guide.pdf`.

To reiterate some facts, each workload is unique and sizing guidelines are projections based on estimation and approximation in an ideal world. In real-world scenarios, I recommend leveraging vRealize Operations Manager or similar third-party tools to monitor capacity utilization post deployment. This will aid as further endorsement for the sizing guidelines or can point out specific issues or workloads that need additional resources.

Virtual SAN sizing utility

Virtual SAN sizing utility is an important tool that provides a very intuitive and interactive methodology of deducing design. This eases much of the sizing and design complexities that an architect goes through. Outlined here are the assumptions based on which the utility decides whether or not the following are true:

- Server hardware and specifications in the cluster are identical
- Workloads hosted have similar characteristics and attributes
- Uniform and identical policies are used across the VSAN cluster

This utility is available at `http://virtualsansizing.vmware.com/go/`.

Prior to delving into the utility, there are two fields that are populated with default values. These are `Number of failures to tolerate` and `Number of disk stripes per object,` and these fields attribute to the performance and availability of the virtual machines. They are discussed in greater detail in *Chapter 5, Truly Software-defined, Policy-based Management*. For the purpose of simplicity, we leave these fields with default values for this exercise.

A set of inputs is provided based on the proposed environment, similar to the following screenshot:

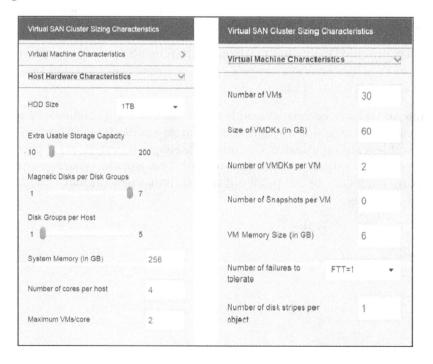

This involves a two-step process. The first step involves providing inputs for the following virtual machine characteristics:

- `Number of VMs`
- `Size of VMDKs (in GB)`
- `Number of VMDKs per VM`
- `Number of Snapshots per VM` (this impacts the number of components that would be created)
- `VM Memory Size (in GB)`

The second step involves keying in the configuration of a typical server.

 Ensure that this is on VMware HCL. You may use any default hardware specifications from a vendor of your choice.

This yields a guideline similar to the following diagram with the minimum supported Virtual SAN configuration to carve out the required infrastructure.

Think of this as a "what-if" scenario where you can increase or decrease the specifications to arrive at different designs catering to business or application needs.

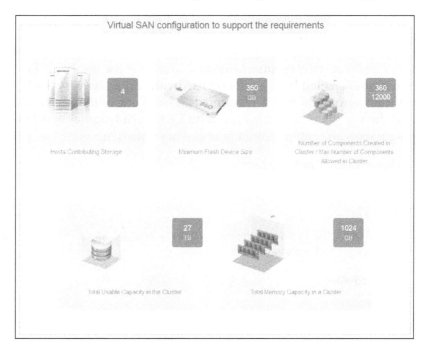

In this example, based on the user inputs as requirements, the proposed design for the VSAN cluster will require four hosts contributing storage. The total usage capacity in the cluster is 27 TB and the minimum flash device capacity per disk group is estimated to be 350 GB. The preceding scenario is an example with random inputs.

In a real-world scenario, an administrator can design the complete VSAN cluster with these two easy steps.

Virtual SAN shapes and sizes

Once we establish the cluster capacity requirements, the next logical step is to finalize the hardware. As discussed in the previous chapters, we have three options to choose from:

- **Custom built**: Build your own Virtual SAN by choosing server hardware, I/O controller, flash devices, and magnetic disks, installing vSphere 5.5, and enabling VSAN

- **VSAN ready nodes**: Choose from a package of pretested and validated hardware from partner vendors

- **EVO: RAIL**: Procure a prepackaged appliance that is plug-and-play.

One of first questions customers have when getting started with VSAN is whether they can repurpose the existing hardware, that is, they have been using vSphere traditionally for a few generations of the product and are looking to migrate to VSAN without changing the underlying hardware. While this is quite possible, VSAN brings certain specific requirements and caveats at the hardware layer. This may not be entirely satisfied by the existing hardware, or, at the very least, may need a significant amount of part replacements. This is one of the key reasons why VMware and their partners have come up with VSAN ready nodes and EVO: RAIL so that configuration and interoperability issues are ironed out.

Let's take a closer look at these options.

Custom built

The Custom built option allows you to construct the components of VSAN. The four components that need to be chosen are:

- Server hardware
- I/O controller
- HDD
- SSD

The server hardware is a no-brainer. You are likely to have gone through this drill in the past while building a non-VSAN setup as well. The VMware hardware compatibility list outlines various different server hardware vendors and their supported, tested, and certified hardware make and model on which the vSphere suite of products can be deployed. For VSAN, the requirement is that the server hardware can be chosen in a similar fashion.

The I/O controller, SSD, and HDD, however, have an important role to play in the VSAN architecture. The following URL is for the VSAN-specific compatibility list:

```
http://www.vmware.com/resources/compatibility/search.
php?deviceCategory=vsan
```

I/O controllers listed in HCL imply that they support "pass through mode" or "RAID 0" (or both). It is recommended to choose a controller with a higher queue depth for performance reasons, while any supported controller has a minimum queue depth of 256 or more.

Similarly, for hard disk drives, an array of options are presented. For SSD, in particular, alongside the generic capacity and other specifications, the class of performance and endurance are also defined in HCL. This is particularly useful to understand the classes of SSD.

Similar to server hardware, there is no explicit compatibility requirement for **Network Interface Cards** (**NICs**) other than the standard HCL. However, there is a very strong recommendation to use 10 GB cards over the 1 GB cards. This is because VM I/O will traverse over the VSAN network in certain conditions and there is significant performance dependency on the throughput of the VSAN network.

VSAN ready nodes

Deducing from the workload profiles defined earlier, each of the partner vendors have prescribed a specific hardware configuration that has been optimized. In other words, once the workload profile and requirements are outlined, you can skip over to the VSAN ready matrix available in VMware HCL, pick a vendor, and choose from an array of available hardware. Currently, Cisco, Dell, Fujitsu, Hewlett Packard, Hitachi, Huawei, IBM, and Supermicro are the vendors, and these are obviously subject to change with partners making amendments to their specifications and newer partners joining the list.

Outlined here is an abstract from the VSAN ready nodes matrix:

DELL

Note: Please work with your Dell Sales Representative to quote and order Dell Virtual SAN Ready Nodes in the US using the **DellStar Solution ID** on the DellStar System. For EMEA and APJ, you can build your order on the DellStar System based on the Ready Node tables below.

High		
Up to 14.4TB raw capacity, 60 Virtual Machines		
Components	Details	QTY
DellStar Solution ID	High 4496251	
SYSTEM	PowerEdge R820, Intel Xeon E5-46XX v2 Processors	1
CPU	Intel Xeon E5-4650 v2 2.4GHz, 25M Cache, 8.0GT/s QPI, Turbo, 10C, 95W, Max Mem 1866MHz	2
MEM	16GB RDIMM, 1866MT/s, Standard Volt, Dual Rank, x4 Data Width	24
SSD	700GB P420M MLC PCIe Solid State Storage Card-Assumes System Warranty up to 5 Years; Not Extendable Past 5 years	2
HDD	1.2TB 10K RPM SAS 6Gbps 2.5in Hot-plug Hard Drive	12
Controller	PERC H710P Integrated RAID Controller, 1GB NV Cache	1
NIC	Intel X520 DP 10Gb DA/SFP+, + I350 DP 1Gb Ethernet, Network Daughter Card	1
USB/SD	Internal Dell SD Module with 8GB SD for ESXi install	1
Virtual Machine Profile: 2 vCPU, 6 GB Memory, 2 x 60 GB virtual disks		

Note that the classification and hardware specifications are already inline with the VMware compatibility guide. No additional validation is needed apart from deciding the number of nodes you need in a cluster.

EVO: RAIL

Each EVO: RAIL appliance is a 2U 4-Node x86 server system with the following configuration. Each node contains:

- Dual Ivy Bridge processors
- 192 GB of memory
- 3 x 1.2 TB HDD for the Virtual SAN disk group
- 1 x 400 GB flash SDD for Virtual SAN read/write cache
- 2 x 10 GbE network ports (SFP+ or RJ-45)
- Boot device (either a boot drive or SATADOM) for ESXi

VMware guidelines for sizing and assumptions

Each appliance can accommodate the following:

- Approximately 100 general purpose virtual machines with a VM profile of 2 vCPU, 4 GB vMEM, and 60 GB vDisk with redundancy

- Up to 250 horizon view virtual desktops with a desktop profile of 2 vCPU, 2 GB vMEM, and 32 GB vDisk with linked clone

Each appliance comprises of four independent nodes sharing dual redundant power supplies; this can scale out to 16 nodes. Scaling out implies adding a second/third/fourth appliance to the first as the appliance discovery is seamless.

The following are the current qualified EVO: RAIL partners (QEP) as of March 2015:

- Dell
- EMC
- Fujitsu
- Hitachi Data Systems
- HP
- NetApp
- Supermicro
- Net One Systems
- Inspur

More partners are expected to join this list.

In summary, the key differentiators of EVO: RAIL that make it very lucrative for customers are as follows:

- The appliance comes embedded with the EVO: RAIL engine that takes care of deployment, configuration, and upgrades to the components such as vSphere, vCenter, and the engine software itself, instead of depending on the update manager

- It is sold as a single SKU by the qualified EVO: RAIL partners

- Its SKU includes hardware, software, service, and support for three years

- The software includes vSphere Enterprise Plus, vCenter Server (Linux-based appliance), Virtual SAN, and vCenter Log Insight

- With EVO: RAIL, there is no such thing as an interoperability or compatibility issue!

If you have been a data center administrator working with multiple vendors and have been on late night bridge calls, the preceding line is invaluable.

Summary

As demonstrated in this chapter, a VSAN-backed architecture can provide a very agile platform. While we discussed capacity management and considerations to be made in a VSAN-backed infrastructure, it is evident that a custom built infrastructure requires significant planning and sizing, while the VSAN ready nodes and EVO: RAIL are ready-made components that can be leveraged as plug-and-play.

The primary reason for building your custom VSAN is a situation wherein you need to repurpose your existing infrastructure. If procuring newer hardware is not a constraint, a much easier option is to pick VSAN ready nodes or, even better, to go the EVO: RAIL way.

In the next chapter, we will discuss the Virtual SAN installation and configuration lifecycle through a deployment performed on a VSAN compliant server.

4
Getting Started with VSAN – Installation and Configuration

In the previous chapter, we discussed the types of workloads and considerations to be made while choosing the right platform for VSAN that meets your business needs. In this chapter, we will deploy a simple setup that will demonstrate the workflow of a typical VSAN deployment.

This chapter aims at:

- Getting a look and feel for the form factors/hardware components
- Familiarizing yourself with the installation and configuration of a VSAN setup
- Providing hands-on experience and getting started with using the product

The finer details of configuration and design considerations will be discussed in the later chapters.

Key concepts

Earlier, we touched upon disk groups and network requirements. Let's revisit them and add more context to how they impact the VSAN cluster.

Disk groups

Disk groups, as we defined earlier, are containers of a set ratio of SSDs to HDDs. Each disk group should have one SSD and a minimum of one HDD. The number of HDDs can be increased up to a maximum of seven per disk group. The aggregate of these disk groups from all the hosts in the cluster that contribute storage form a single large VSAN datastore. The composition of the disk group in particular plays a very important role in the performance outcome in a VSAN cluster.

SSDs contribute to performance and HDDs contribute to capacity. A higher ratio of SSD to HDD improves the performance, while the typical requirement is to have at least 10 percent SSDs. The role of SSDs is to accelerate the I/O throughput. The capacity of SSDs is split into two, 70 percent for read caching and 30 percent for write buffering.

Hence, if there is more than one SSD, you can create multiple disk groups and increase the cache capacity per disk group. While doing so, you also automatically mitigate the single point of failure, that is, in our test setup, we have two SSDs from each host that can be leveraged to form two disk groups per host, and we can associate two HDDs per disk group. If there is a single SSD failure, only the data on that disk group is impacted, while the other disk group is fully functional.

Note that with VSAN 6.0, there is an architectural change and an all flash-backed VSAN datastore is supported. We will discuss this and other new features in *Chapter 9, What's New in VSAN 6.0?*.

Virtual SAN network

A VSAN network is a unique network traffic requirement for VSAN to operate. For this purpose, a new type of VMkernel, Portgroup, has been introduced with vSphere 5.5. This is a proprietary protocol and the specifications have not been published by VMware.

Primarily, the VSAN traffic comprises of:

- **Multicast traffic**: A layer two multicast for heartbeat exchange between VSAN nodes and metadata updates is sent through the VSAN network
- **Storage traffic**: Whenever an I/O needs to traverse to "objects" located on other nodes (non-local disk), it is sent through the VSAN network

All hosts participating in a Virtual SAN cluster should ideally be on a single level two network with multicast enabled. The same requirement holds good if the VSAN network spans across layer 3 network. The implementation will need to be assessed alongside network vendors/administrators to cater to the specific features and security requirements.

Prerequisite checklist

For the purpose of end-to-end understanding of the VSAN architecture, we will leverage "build your own" methodology, also known as the "custom built" methodology, to build the VSAN cluster. In this methodology, we go the whole nine yards of choosing each component of VSAN, ensure that it's on HCL, and build the VSAN cluster.

Here is a simplified checklist of the requirements:

- Ensure that the server hardware is on VMware HCL

- Minimum of three ESXi 5.5 U1(or higher version) with at least one HDD and one SDD, a controller that supports pass through mode or RAID-0 and at least 1 GB network card.

- Hosts should be managed by a vCenter 5.5 U1 (or higher)

- Boot device for ESXi USD, SD card, local storage, or boot from SAN

- Minimum 6 GB of RAM per host

- Multicast traffic needs to be enabled at the physical switch

- You can choose to use the evaluation license for testing purposes

Installation workflow

The installation workflow can be broken down into five phases as defined here. While it is common to check the hardware compatibility list prior to deployment, there is some added significance to specific components that need to be validated through HCL for VSAN, otherwise the steps of the first two phases are no different from any greenfield deployment in a vSphere-backed infrastructure, and the rest of the phases are very specific to VSAN deployment. The following image shows the phases of installation workflow:

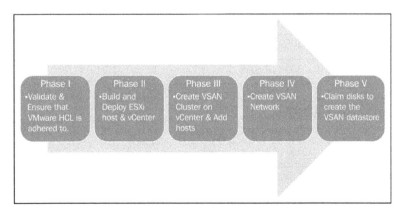

The phases in an installation workflow are as follows:

- **Phase I**: This ensures that all the components of VSAN are qualified, certified, and listed in VMware HCL. This phase is to further underline the importance of this installation.

- **Phase II**: The second phase involves ESXi and vCenter installation. From a VSAN perspective, there are no additional packages or **vSphere installation bundles** (**VIBs**) that need to be added. VSAN is a natively embedded feature and only requires to be enabled and configured.

- **Phase III**: Once the ESXi hosts and vCenter are set up successfully, the third phase involves creating a cluster similar to the HA/DRS cluster. We additionally enable Virtual SAN while creating a cluster.

- **Phase IV**: This phase involves carving out the necessary network requirements for facilitating Virtual SAN. You can also choose to automate the VSAN datastore creation.

- **Phase V**: If you have not chosen to fully automate the VSAN datastore creation, this final phase is an additional step in the process to aggregate all the local disks to create a single large VSAN datastore.

Hardware specifications

Outlined here are the hardware specifications that we will use in this test setup. These specifications are aligned with the requirements and prerequisites:

Component	Make and model
Server hardware	Dell PowerEdge R720xd - 2U rack
Controller	PERC H710P Integrated RAID controller
Memory	64 GB
CPU	Intel Xeon E5-2620 v2
Solid State Disk	2 x 400 GB SSD
Hard Disk Drives	4 x 300 GB SAS
Network Interface Card	2 x Broadcom Corporation NetXtreme II BCM57810 10 Gigabit Ethernet 4 x Broadcom Corporation NetXtreme BCM5720 Gigabit Ethernet
Boot Device	SanDisk Cruzer 32 GB USB Device

Server node

In data center terminology, server dimensions are depicted in rack units, that is, the form factors (width, height, and depth per unit) are standardized and servers are classified as 1U, 2U, and so on, to reflect the dimensions of the specific make and model. Here is a pictorial representation of an actual server node that we use in our setup to build the VSAN cluster; Dell PowerEdge R720xd is a 2U server:

Server hardware used as a VSAN node

Cluster layout

We have a three-node cluster, each with two SSDs and four HDDs, effectively contributing two disk groups per host; thereby, we cumulatively have six disk groups to create a VSAN datastore.

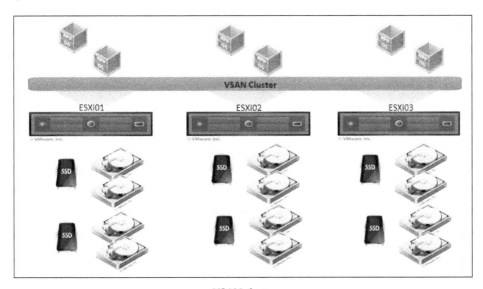

VSAN cluster

Network layout

The networking required for Virtual SAN is set up on a vSwitch for simplicity. We have three vSwitches created with the six network cards distributed to the required port groups, as shown in the following table:

vSwitch	NIC	Speed	Type
vSwitch0	vmnic0 vmnic1	2 x 1 GB	Management and vMotion network (vmk0)
vSwitch1	vmnic2 vmnic3	2 x 10 GB	VSAN network (vmk1)
vSwitch2	vmnic4 vmnic5	2 x 1 GB	Virtual machine network

Setting up a VSAN cluster

Presuming that administrators are familiar with ESXi and vCenter installation, we will skip the basic vSphere installation process. For additional reference and guidance, kindly refer to *vSphere Installation and Setup Guide* available at https:// www.vmware.com/support/pubs/vsphere-esxi-vcenter-server-pubs.html.

One interesting discussion point is how to build the vCenter VM that needs to reside within the VSAN datastore, since vCenter is required to enable VSAN. This argument holds good specifically in a greenfield deployment, since there is no existing platform where vCenter can be built to bootstrap a VSAN deployment. This becomes a classic "chicken and egg" situation. The solution is to essentially bootstrap VSAN without vCenter. The procedure is explained at http://www.vmware.com/ files/pdf/products/vsan/VMware-TechNote-Bootstrapping-VSAN-without-vCenter.pdf.

Barring this complication, VSAN configuration is fairly straightforward. You can either create a VSAN-enabled cluster and add hosts, or enable VSAN on an existing cluster; the former is preferred. In case you need to enable it on an existing cluster, you will need to disable high availability in the cluster first. It is also important to note that VSAN claims only unused and empty disks. Disks that were previously used for some other purposes are deemed as ineligible. We will need to wipe out any stale partition information existing on the disks to claim and append to a disk group. These are explained in *Chapter 8, Troubleshooting and Monitoring Utilities for Virtual SAN.* As previously discussed, it is not mandatory for all the hosts to contribute to storage. Some hosts may be added to a VSAN cluster to increase the computation capacity.

Again, to keep things simple, we will start creating the VSAN cluster from scratch:

1. Connect to the vCenter server through the vSphere web client.

2. Create a new cluster, as shown in the following screenshot:

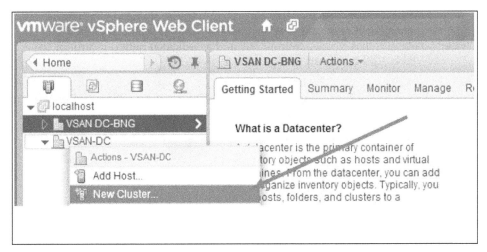

Create a new cluster through web client

3. Enable Virtual SAN and leave it as **Automatic** for the **Add disks to storage** option, as shown here:

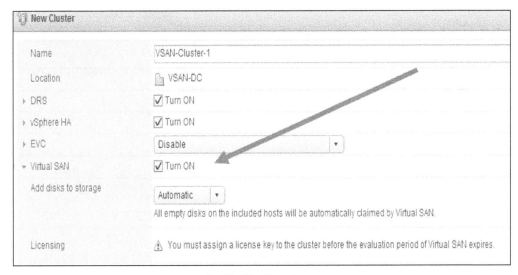

Enable VSAN on cluster

4. Add hosts to the cluster.

5. Create a vSwitch with a VMKernel port enabled with Virtual SAN traffic on each host that is added to the cluster.

 While it is possible to enable Virtual SAN traffic alongside ESXi hosts' management networks, it is recommended to provide a dedicated network, that is, a separate VLAN and a dedicated network card for the VSAN VMkernel port group.

6. As shown in the following screenshot, a distinct new VMkernel port group type has been introduced called **Virtual SAN traffic**:

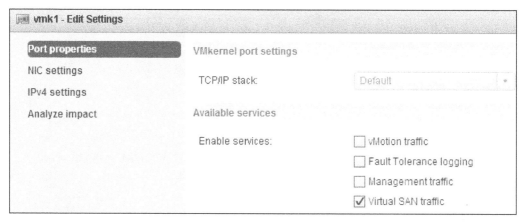

Enable VSAN Traffic

7. Verify that all disks have been claimed and are in use. In this example, we have two SSDs and four magnetic disks per host:

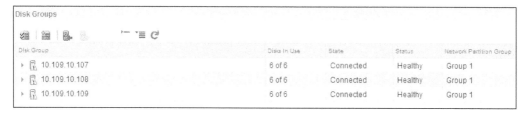

Disks claimed

8. Navigate to the datastore view and verify whether a VSAN datastore of the expected size is created, as shown here:

VSAN datastore validation

Virtual SAN aggregates all disk groups to carve out a single datastore that is created when you enable Virtual SAN.

Virtual SAN is perfectly capable of claiming available devices to form the VSAN datastore. This can be done automatically by setting the VSAN cluster to the **Automatic** mode, as explained in the preceding example. This will also ensure that if there are newer hosts/disks appended to the cluster, they will be claimed by VSAN without any additional user configuration. However, if there are any circumstances in which the administrator would like to control this process, the setting can be switched to the **Manual** mode. One key reason to leverage the manual mode is to have granular control to govern the disk group creation and the SSD to HDD ratio.

Disks associated with Virtual SAN cannot be used as RDMs or for creating VMFS volumes.

In the following example, we demonstrate disk group creation in **Manual** mode. For the sake of consistency, Virtual SAN configuration settings are performed at the cluster level and not at the host level:

1. Right-click on the cluster.

2. Browse to **Disk Management** under **Virtual SAN**.

3. Click on **Claims Disks**.

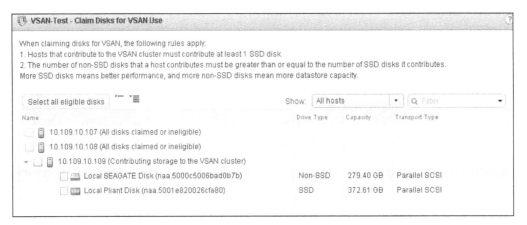

Claim disks

 Note that there will be a clear distinction between SSD and non-SSD disks outlined as **Drive Type**. However, there have been instances where the SSD disks were not detected correctly and needed to be explicitly detected; refer to the VMware KB at `http://kb.vmware.com/kb/2008938`.

This completes the VSAN cluster setup and you can start creating virtual machines.

The following points will be discussed in more detail in *Chapter 7, Design Considerations and Guidelines*:

• The preceding setup is based on **vNetwork Standard Switch** (**vSS**) for easier understanding. The recommended design would be to leverage **vNetwork Distributed Switch** (**vDS**).

• Segregating VSAN traffic through the use of VLANs is a good practice.

• vDS natively provides consistency and also advanced features such as NIOC for better throughput management.

• VSAN license also packages vDS features irrespective of the vSphere license procured.

- Host profiles are recommended to ensure consistency and ease of deployment.
- IPv6 is currently not supported.
- If the ESXi host memory exceeds 512 GB, the installation needs to be on a magnetic disk and not on a USB or SD card.

VSAN ready nodes – installation

VSAN ready nodes installation is made relatively easy by removing the Phase I process of VMware HCL validation. The Phases from II to V remain the same:

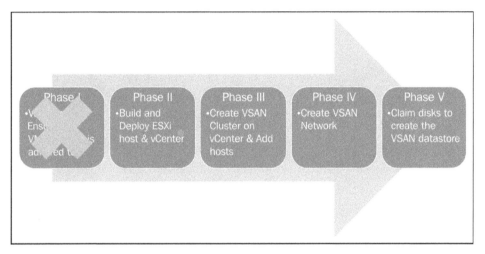

Workflow for VSAN ready nodes

Summary

In this chapter, we demonstrated a simple installation and configuration of Virtual SAN. We discussed this in phases to segregate the standard vSphere components installation (which is outside the scope of this book) and Virtual SAN-specific configuration steps.

Also, the hardware leveraged is compliant with VSAN to underline the importance of compatibility. While this is a simple installation aimed at getting started with VSAN, we will look into the optimizations and best practices to strive toward the perfect design and setup in *Chapter 7, Design Considerations and Guidelines*.

From the chapters covered so far, you should now be familiar with the basic concepts of Virtual SAN and understand the constraints and considerations with regards to capacity management in Virtual SAN. Finally, you should be able to set up and deploy a simple Virtual SAN-backed cluster with n nodes.

With the VSAN datastore now created, the stage is set to effectively deploy virtual machines from a software defined storage perspective. In the next chapter, we will discuss the finer details of virtual machine deployment on a VSAN datastore and the significance of policies.

5
Truly Software-defined, Policy-based Management

In this chapter, we will discuss one of the key characteristics of Virtual SAN called **Storage Policy Based Management (SPBM)**.

Traditionally, storage capabilities are tiered and provisioned. Some of the key attributes for tiering are performance, capacity, and availability. The actual implementation of tiers is performed at the hardware level, governed by physical disk capabilities and RAID configuration. VSAN, however, establishes the capabilities at the software layer through policies.

Here we will closely review:

- Why is SPBM used?
- Attributes that are configurable through SPBM
- Understand how SPBM works

Overall, we will discuss the various permutations and combinations of the policy-based management of storage, and how this method modernizes storage provisioning and paves the way for being truly software-defined.

Why do we need policies?

Back in the '90s, Gartner discussed tiered storage architecture with traditional storage arrays. Devices were tiered based on their cost and data on certain factors such as criticality, age, performance, and a few others. This meant that some data made their way to the fastest and most reliable tier and other data into slower and less expensive ones. This tiering was done at the device level, that is, the storage administrator segmented devices based on cost or there was heterogeneous storage presented to servers varying between high-end, mid-end, and low-end arrays. An administrator would then manually provision data on the respective tiers. There have been several advancements with storage arrays automating tiering at the array level.

With virtualization however, data seldom static and the ability to move data around through features such as Storage vMotion gave the right level of agility to the vSphere administrators. The flip side of this is that it became very error prone and difficult to maintain compliance. For example, during maintenance tasks, a high I/O intensive virtual machine may be migrated to a low IOPS capable datastore; this would silently lead to a performance issue for the application and overall user experience.

Hence, there was a need for a very high degree of control, automation, and a VM-centric approach to satisfy each virtual machine's storage requirements. The solution for this problem is SPBM. With SPBM, we are able to build very granular policies to each VMDK associated to a virtual machine and these policies follow the virtual machine wherever they go.

Understanding SPBM

An SPBM policy can be thought of as a blueprint or plan that outlines the storage performance, capacity and availability requirement of a virtual machine. The policy is then associated with individual objects (VMDK). These policies are then applied by replicating, distributing and caching the objects.

The concept of objects is discussed in greater detail in *Chapter 6, Architecture Overview*. At this juncture, it suffices to understand that objects are parts of a virtual machine; a virtual machine disk (VMDK) and the snapshot delta files are examples of objects.

Let's discuss this with an example of RAID 0 concept. In RAID 0, data is striped, that is, data is broken down into blocks and each block is written on a different disk drives/controller in the RAID group so that, cumulative IOPS of all disks in the RAID group are efficiently used, and this in turn increases the performance. Similarly, we can define a policy with SPBM for an object (VMDK) that will stripe the object across a VSAN datastore.

It is mandatory for each virtual machine that is to be deployed on a VSAN datastore to be associated with a policy. If one has not been defined, a default, predefined policy will be applied.

In a nutshell, the capabilities of VSAN datastore will be abstracted and presented in such a way that an object can distinctly be placed adhering to very specific needs of the specific object. All this, while another virtual machines' objects resid on the same VSAN datastore, can have a totally different set of capabilities.

An important component that enables this abstraction is **vStorage APIs for Storage Awareness (VASA)**; more details on VASA are discussed at the end of this chapter.

The communication workflow is as follows:

- Define the capabilities required for a VM in a storage policy in vCenter
- Policy information is cascaded to VSAN through VASA
- VASA assesses whether VSAN can accommodate the capability requirement and reports compliance on a per-storage object basis

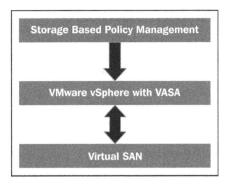

Let's understand this concept with a simple example. Consider a fileserver virtual machine that comprises of two VMDKs or objects, one of which is for the OS and the other where the actual data is being read from or written to by several users. The OS VMDK requires lower IOPS capability, while the other VMDK is very I/O intensive and requires a significantly faster disk.

The application team that maintains this server demands this workload to be placed in a tier 1 datastore, which in turn translates to a LUN from a mid-range or high-end array, the cost of which obviously is rather high. A vSphere administrator can argue that the OS VMDK can be part of a tier 2 or tier 3 VMFS datastore that is less expensive, whereas the database VMDK can be placed on a Tier 1 datastore to meet the business SLAs for storage optimization.

While this is theoretically achievable, in reality it possesses significant administrative overheads and a serious sore-point if there are any failures in the datastore where the files reside. Troubleshooting and restoring the VM to the running state will be quite a cumbersome and time-consuming task. Now imagine if a policy is able to cater to the storage requirements of this VM, an administrator carves out a policy as per the requirements and associates it to the VM's objects residing on the VSAN datastore. After this one-time effort, the policy ensures that the virtual machine is compliant with the demands of the application team throughout its lifecycle.

Another interesting and useful feature of SPBM is that during the lifecycle of the virtual machine, the administrator can amend the policies and reapply without disruption or downtime.

To summarize, with Storage Policy Based Management, the virtual machine deployment is tied to the Virtual SAN capabilities and thereby removes the administrative overhead and complication associated with manually building this setup.

VSAN datastore capabilities

VSAN datastore capabilities help define the performance, availability, reliability, and the capabilities indirectly governing the capacity consumed by an object. Let's dive into the specific capabilities that can be abstracted and managed.

The following is a list of capabilities that can be defined on a VSAN datastore:

- Number of disk stripes per object
- Number of failures to tolerate
- Flash read cache reservation
- Force provisioning
- Object space reservation

Accessing the VSAN datastore capabilities

We can access these capabilities through the vSphere web client as described in the following steps and screenshots:

1. Connect to the vCenter server through the vSphere web client.

2. Navigate to **Home | VM Storage Policies**, as shown here:

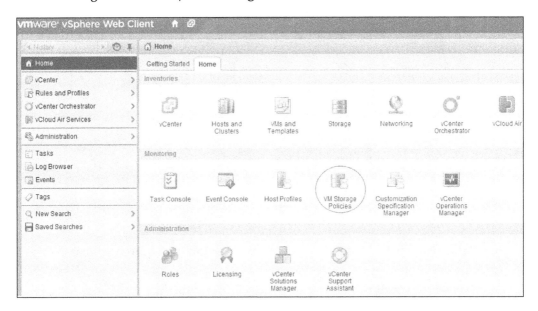

3. Choose **VSAN** from the dropdown for **Rules based on vendor specific capabilities**.

4. Create (or edit) a VM storage policy, as shown in the following screenshot:

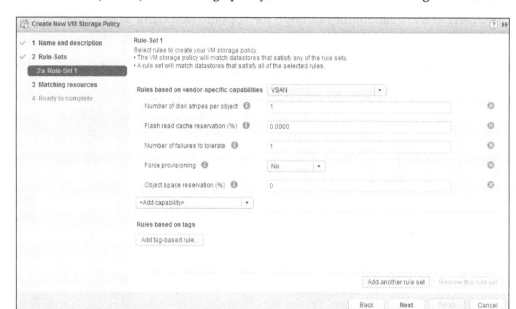

5. Define **Rule Set** of the policy describing the storage requirements of an object.

6. Review the configuration settings and click on **Finish**.

Number of disk stripes per object

This capability simulates the traditional RAID 0 concept by defining the number of physical disks across which each replica of a storage object is striped. In a typical RAID 0, this means that there is concurrent and parallel I/O running into multiple disks. However, in the context of VSAN, this raises a few questions.

Consider this typical scenario:

- A disk group can have a maximum of one SSD
- All I/O read cache and write buffer are routed first to SSD
- I/O is then destaged from SSD to magnetic disks

How will having more stripes improve performance if SSD intercepts all I/O?

The answer to this question is that it depends, and cannot be administratively controlled. However, at a high level, performance improvement can be witnessed. If the structure of the object is spread across magnetic disks from different hosts in the cluster, then multiple SSDs and magnetic disks will be used. This is very similar to the traditional RAID 0. Another influencing factor is how I/O moves from SSD to magnetic disks. We will discuss the I/O flow in greater detail in the next chapter where we will discuss in what cases the disk striping in VSAN helps specifically in terms of read and write I/Os.

 Number of disk stripes per object is by default 1. There can be a maximum of 12 stripes per object.

Number of failures to tolerate

This capability defines the availability requirements of the object. In this context, the nature of failure can be at host, network, and disk level in the cluster. Based on the value defined for the number of failures to tolerate (n), there are $n+1$ replicas that are built to sustain n failures. It is important to understand that the object can sustain n concurrent failures, that is, all permutations and combinations of host, network, and/or disk-level failures can be sustained until n failures. This is similar to a RAID 1 mirroring concept, albeit replicas are placed on different hosts.

 Number of failures to tolerate is by default set to 1. We can have a maximum value of 3.

Scenario based examples

Outlined here are three scenarios demonstrating the placements of components of an object. Note that objects are of four types. For easier understanding, we will discuss scenarios based on the VMDK object. We'll sample VMDK since these are the most sensitive and relevant in the context of objects on the VSAN datastore. In addition, these are some illustrations of how VSAN may place the objects by adhering to the policies defined, and this may vary depending on resource availability and layout specific to each deployment.

Scenario 1

Number of failures to tolerate is equal to 1.

In the first scenario, we have crafted a simple policy to tolerate one failure. The virtual machine objects are expected to have a mirrored copy and the objective is to eliminate a single point of failure. The typical use for this policy is an operating system VMDK:

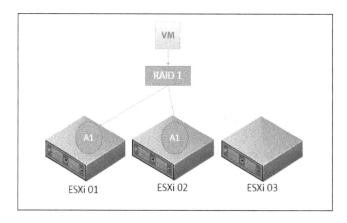

Scenario 2

Number of failures to tolerate is equal to 1.

Number of disk stripes per object is equal to 2.

In this scenario, we increase the stripe width of the object, while keeping the failure tolerance left at 1. The objective here is to improve the performance as well as ensure that there is no single point of failure. The expected layout is as shown here; the object is mirrored and striped:

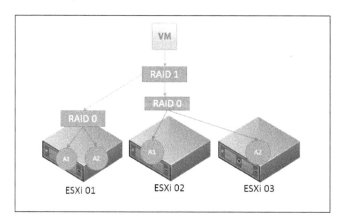

Scenario 3

Number of failures to tolerate is equal to 2.

Number of disk stripes per object is equal to 2.

Extending from the preceding scenario, we increase the failure tolerance level to 2. Effectively, two mirrors can fail, so the layout will expand as illustrated in the following diagram. Note that to facilitate *n* failures, you would need *2n+1* nodes.

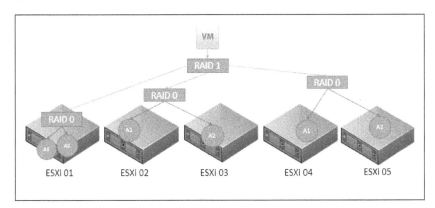

An administrator can validate the actual physical disk placement of the components, that is, the parts that make up the object from the virtual machines' **Manage** tab from the vSphere web client. Navigate to **VM** | **Manage** | **VM Storage Policies**:

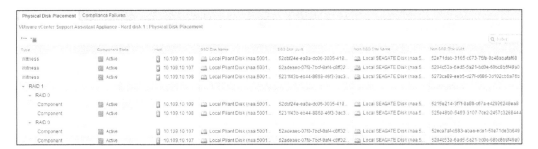

Flash read cache reservation

By default, all virtual machine objects based on demand share the read cache available from the flash device that is part of each disk group. However, there may be scenarios wherein specific objects require reserved read cache, typically for a read intensive workload that needs to have the maximum amount of its reads to be serviced by a flash device.

In such cases, an administrator can explicitly define a percentage of flash cache to be reserved for the object. The flash read cache reservation capability defines the amount of flash capacity that will be reserved/blocked for the storage object to be used as read cache. The reservation is displayed as a percentage of the object. You can have a minimum of 0 percent and can go up to 100 percent, that is, you can reserve the entire object size on the flash disk for read cache. For purposes of granularity, since the flash device may run into terabytes of capacity, the value for flash cache can be specified up to 4 decimal places; for example, it can be set to 0.0001 percent.

As with any reservation concept, blocking resources for one object implies the resource is unavailable for another object. Therefore, unless there is a specific need, this should be left at default and Virtual SAN should be allowed to have control over the allocation. This will ensure adequate capacity distribution between objects.

[The default value is 0 percent and the maximum value is 100 percent.]

Force provisioning

We create policies to ensure that the storage requirements of a virtual machine object is strictly adhered to. In the event that the VSAN datastore cannot satisfy the storage requirements specified by the policy, the virtual machine will not be provisioned. This capability allows for a strict compliance check. However, it may also become an obstacle when you need to urgently deploy virtual machines but the datastore does not satisfy the storage requirements of the virtual machine.

The force provisioning capability allows an administrator to override this behavior. By default, **Force Provisioning** is set to **No**. By toggling this setting to **Yes**, virtual machines can be forcefully provisioned. It is important to understand that an administrator should remediate the constraints that lead to provisioning failing in the first place.

[It has a boolean value, which is set to **No** by default.]

Object space reservation

Virtual machines provisioned on Virtual SAN are, by default, provisioned as thin disks. The **Object Space Reservation** parameter defines the logical size of the storage object or, in other words, whether the specific object should remain thin, partially, or fully allocated. While this is not entirely new and is similar to the traditional practice of either thin provisioning or thick provisioning a VMDK, VSAN provides a greater degree of control by letting the vSphere administrators choose the percentage of disk that should be thick provisioned.

 The default value is 0 percent and maximum value is 100 percent.

Under the hood – SBPM

It is important to understand how the abstraction works under the hood in order to surface the Virtual SAN capabilities, which in turn help to create and associate policies to virtual machines. The following section about VASA and managing storage providers is informative, and for better understanding; you may not run into a situation where you need to make any configuration changes to storage providers.

vSphere APIs for Storage Awareness

To understand VASA better, let's consider a scenario wherein an administrator is deploying a virtual machine on a traditional SAN array. He would need to choose the appropriate datastore to suit the capabilities and requirements of the virtual machine or certain business requirements. For instance, there could be workloads that need to be deployed in a tier 1 LUN. The existing practice is to ensure that the right virtual machine gets deployed on the right datastore; there were rather archaic styles of labelling, or simply asking the administrator the capability of the LUN. Now, replace this methodology with a mechanism to identify the storage capabilities through API. VASA provides such a capability and aids in identifying the specific attributes of the array and passes on these capabilities to vCenter. This implies that a vSphere administrator can have end-to-end visibility through a single management plane of vCenter.

Storage DRS, storage health, and capacity monitoring, to name a few, are very useful and effective features implemented through VASA. To facilitate VASA, storage array vendors create plugins called vendor/storage providers. These plugins allow storage vendors to publish the capabilities to vCenter, which in turn surfaces it in the UI.

For VMware Virtual SAN, the VSAN storage provider is developed by VMware and built into ESXi hypervisors. By enabling VSAN on a cluster, the plugins get automatically registered with vCenter. The VSAN storage provider surfaces the VSAN datastores' capabilities which in turn is used to create appropriate policies.

Managing Virtual SAN storage providers

Once Virtual SAN is enabled and storage provider registration is complete, an administrator can verify this through the vSphere web client:

1. Navigate to the vCenter server in the vSphere web client.
2. Click on the **Manage** tab, and click on **Storage Providers**.

The expected outcome would be to have one VSAN provider online and the remaining storage providers on standby mode. The following screenshot shows a three-node cluster:

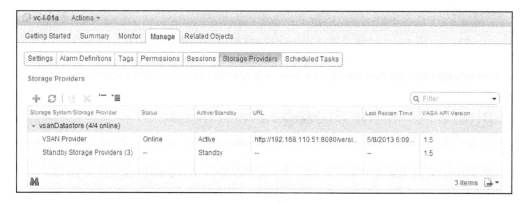

If the host that currently has the online storage provider fails, another host will bring its provider online.

Summary

In this chapter, we discussed the significance of Storage Policy Based Management in detail and how it plays a key factor in defining the storage provisioning at the software layer. We further discussed the VSAN datastore capabilities with scenarios and how it operates under the hood.

In the next chapter, we will dive deeper into the anatomy of I/O and architectural components that make up the Virtual SAN.

6
Architecture Overview

In this chapter, we will understand why VSAN has a relatively complex architecture, and then discuss the structure and components of VSAN.

We will then take a closer look at the finer details of how an I/O is read or written on a VSAN datastore. As we study the anatomy of a VSAN I/O, we will also closely examine the filesystem layout of VMFS-L and its key ingredients.

We will connect the dots on how this hybrid architecture and its derived filesystem structure help in implementing a granular policy specific to the objects. Furthermore, we will mildly touch upon the failure scenarios with VSAN and how the architecture enables data availability.

We will discuss the following topics in this chapter:

- Anatomy of I/O
- Objects, components, and witnesses
- VSAN and high availability

The specific architectural changes with VSAN 6.0 are discussed in *Chapter 9, What's New in VSAN 6.0?*.

Why such an architecture?

Let's take a step back to understand the fundamental reason for the somewhat complex VSAN architecture. While the cost estimates may vary slightly from time to time, it will only proportionally vary.

An enterprise flash device cost per 10 GB is approximately $10, while the cost of a magnetic disk per 10 GB is approximately $1.

In contrast, from an **Input/Output Operations Per Second (IOPS)** perspective, the flash device costs $0.01 per IOPS and a magnetic disk costs $3.

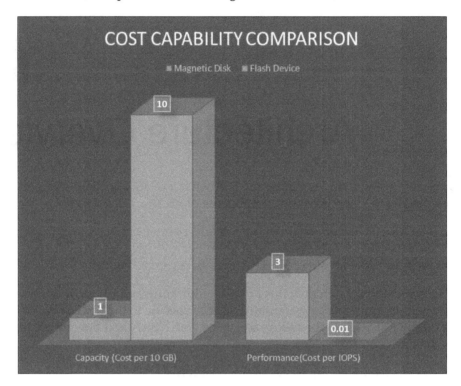

It's not rocket science to realize that the capacity of a magnetic disk is fairly cheap and the cost of IOPS is exponentially cheaper for an SSD.

An architectural model that can leverage the IOPS capabilities of a flash device and storage capacity of the magnetic disk strikes an optimal balance with price and performance. This, of course coupled with the fact that we don't need the luxuries of a fabric infrastructure and a SAN array, means that this architecture exponentially optimizes the price and performance.

VSAN, in essence, uses flash devices to accelerate I/O. At a high level, VSAN aims to have the maximum I/O serviced by the flash device, similar to the workflow illustrated in the following image, although there are likely to be a few cases where we have to perform reads directly from magnetic disks. Such IOPS are also known as *cache misses*. In a nutshell, we get a near-to-flash device performance with just approximately 10 percent of flash to magnetic disk ratio.

Anatomy of I/O

All the virtual machine data is eventually stored in magnetic disks. The only difference is that some are written immediately and some at a later point in time sequentially.

Let's review specific I/O workflows that are associated with VSAN:

- Write buffer
- Data destage
- Read cache

Write buffer

A guest operating system within the virtual machine performs a write operation intended to the virtual disk associated to the virtual machine. The I/O is received by the Virtual SAN module on the localhost of the virtual machine that it is currently running on. On receipt of the I/O, the VSAN knows the replicas of the virtual disk and triggers a parallel write operation to the replicas. The writes are performed first on the flash devices that frontend the magnetic disks holding the replicas. Once the I/O completes on all the flash devices, an acknowledgement is sent back to the guest OS that the I/O is complete.

The data written on the flash device is eventually retired/destaged to the final destination, that is, the magnetic disk.

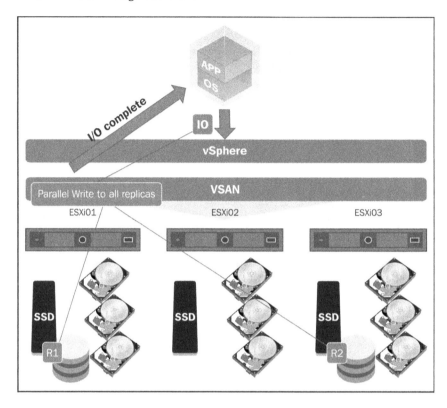

Destaging data to a magnetic disk

The data on a flash device is temporary, which is why it is known as the write buffer. There are further optimizations on how the data written on flash is transferred to the magnetic disk. Outlined here are the optimizations:

- There is no specific time frame or frequency based on which data is destaged. This is based on an internal algorithm of Virtual SAN.

- Until the data resides in SSD, it is subject to modification and overwrites by the guest OS/VM.

- Only the final cut of data is to be written to the magnetic disk; multiple iterations prior to this need not be destaged.

- Data destage occurs in batches, that is, blocks in close proximity are destaged in a batch. This batchwise destaging simulates sequential I/O, which further optimizes the magnetic disk IOPS.

Let's evaluate these optimizations with an example. Assume that a file of size 100 MB is being written to a VMDK. Subsequently, the file is modified to remove 20 MB of content and shrinks the overall size of the file to 80 MB. Assuming that all of this modification occurs within an interval prior to data destage, only 80 MB of data is destaged to the magnetic disk, thus saving IOPS to the magnetic disk equivalent to adding and removing the 20 MB.

The read cache

To greatly reduce the latency of reading off the magnetic disk, frequently accessed disk blocks of virtual machines are stored in the flash device. A read I/O from a guest OS is received by the VSAN module on the local host where VM is running. VSAN then decides which replica to perform the read from; the replica component may exist on a disk group locally or remotely. Once the replica is chosen and read, the I/O is sent to the host where the replica resides. The read I/O is fetched from the flash device if it exists, or else it's retrieved from the magnetic disk. This read is then potentially cached in flash and serviced back to the guest operating system.

Reads, when fetched from magnetic disks, are deemed cache miss. These will have more latency; however, subsequent reads are faster since they will be cached in SSD. A successful retrieval from flash is deemed a cache hit.

The READ I/O workflow

READ I/O workflow can be summarized as follows:

1. The guest VM initiates read I/O.
2. The VSAN module on the local ESXi host receives read I/O.
3. VSAN decides the replica to which the read I/O should be sent.
4. It then dispatches the request to one of the hosts having the replica.
5. The read I/O is processed from flash cache if found.
6. If not found, relevant data is retrieved from the magnetic disk and stored in flash.
7. The read I/O is serviced back to the guest OS.

The workflow can be represented by the following flowchart:

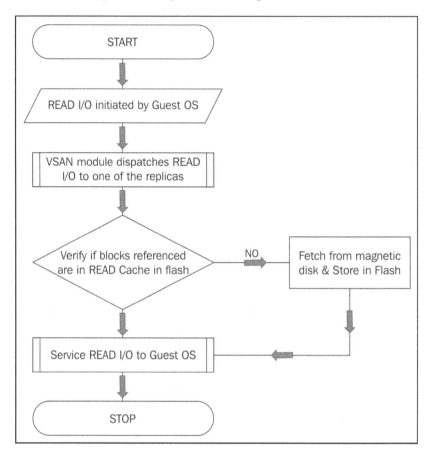

Although the reads dispatched to replicas are generally load balanced, VSAN sensibly sends reads of specific logical block ranges of data to the same replicas. For example, in a given range, the same replica will be found servicing the read and thereby cached on only one flash device in the cluster. It is understood that capacity is expensive with flash. Hence, this mechanism will ensure that flash capacity is conservatively used and there is no redundant read cache content for a specific block range across flash devices in the cluster.

Objects, components, and witnesses

Earlier, we simply stated that the reads/writes are targeted to the virtual disk associated to the guest operating system or VM, while in the conventional VMFS filesystem this is fairly straightforward, as a virtual disk(s) relates to the set of VMDK files.

While this is similar in Virtual SAN from an administrator's perspective, under the covers the mechanism significantly varies. This is because there is a newer set of challenges to be dealt with by VSAN from a software-defined storage perspective. Some of the challenges are policy-based provisioning (availability and performance) and vSphere features that are dependent on shared storage.

These are particularly challenging given that virtual machine data is now confined to local storage.

To address these challenges, VSAN uses a VMFS-derived filesystem called VMFS-L, which is an object-based storage system where objects are distributed across the cluster based on a distributed RAID concept.

What is an object?

An object is a logical volume that contains data and metadata that is distributed across the VSAN cluster. When deploying a virtual machine on a VSAN datastore, VSAN creates an object for each virtual disk and also a container object that stores all the metadata files.

During its lifecycle, a virtual machine will be associated with the following storage objects:

- Swap object
- Virtual disks or VMDKs and snapshot delta-disk objects (actual guest OS/ VMs disk data)
- Virtual machine home namespace

While storage policies are strictly adhered to by VMDK objects and snapshot delta-disk objects, the VM home namespace and swap objects have their own set of defined policies and deviate from the policy aligned to the virtual machine. This is done due to the simple fact that the nature of these objects do not command a reservation for cache or a need for stripe width to be increased.

In the following example, the VSAN-VCSA55U1a(1) virtual machine has the **VM home**, **Hard disk 1** and **Hard disk 2** storage objects, as shown in the following screenshot:

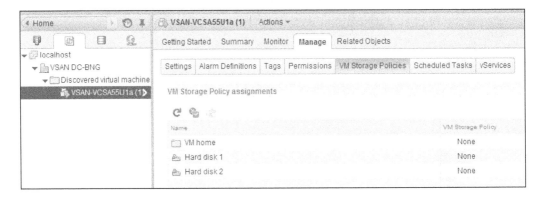

A swap object

A swap is created while the virtual machine is powered on. Its object content and purpose is similar to a traditional swap file (*.vswp) in vSphere. The size of the swap is fully allocated on the disk. Outlined here are the swap file policies which are distinct from the storage policies allocated to the virtual machine. Modifying this policy is not recommended as it may lead to wasted resources and other issues. For instance, a VSWP file is perhaps a fairly irrelevant file that comes into play only during swapping and during severe resource constraints. However, if **Force provisioning** of swap file is set to 0, then VMware HA may fail to restart the VM potentially due to lack of resources for the swap object. In other words, this *not so important* object becomes an impediment for the VM to be powered on. Hence, unlike any other object, **Force provisioning** for the swap object is set to 1 by default. Here are the swap file policies:

- **Number of disk objects to stripe**: The default value is 1.
- **Object space reservation**: The default value is 100 percent.
- **Read cache reservation**: The default value is 0 percent.
- **Number of failures to tolerate**: The default value is 1.
- **Force provisioning**: This is enabled by default.

The virtual machine home namespace

The virtual machine home namespace is an object that contains the rest of the virtual machine files you would traditionally see in the virtual machine directory in vSphere, excluding the swap file and (flat) VMDK.

Here are the set of files that are likely to exist in the VM home namespace:

- The configuration file (*.vmx)
- Virtual machine disk descriptor file (*.vmdk)
- Log files associated to the VM (*.log)
- Memory snapshot file (*.vmsn)

Additionally, the following files may also exist:

- Replication-related files (vSphere Replication and Site Recovery Manager)
- Guest customization files
- Content-based read cache

The policy associated with the VM home namespace has the following settings:

- **Number of disk objects to stripe**: Value of 1
- **Object space reservation**: Value of 0%
- **Read cache reservation**: Value of 0%
- **Number of failures to tolerate**: Inherits storage policy set for the VM
- **Force provisioning**: Inherits storage policy set for the VM

Similar to the swap object, VM home namespace has its own set of default policies, with some of it inherited from the VM's storage policy and some defined particularly in-line with the nature of contents in the namespace. As you can imagine, a file such as VMX will not benefit from stripe width, saving VSAN from the unnecessary complexities and resource utilization. The following screenshot outlines the VM home namespace's physical disk placement:

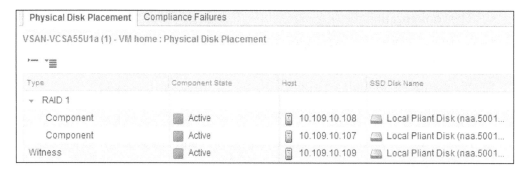

Here, although no policies are associated explicitly, a RAID 1 (FTT = 1) configuration is applied. Two replica components have been created and located on two distinct hosts, and a third witness component is placed on another host that will be discussed shortly.

Virtual disks and snapshot delta-disks

The virtual disk or snapshot delta-disks object holds the actual content of the guest OS, that is, data within the guest operating system are stored here. For obvious reasons, this is the most important object from the VSAN perspective and strictly adheres to the storage policy set for the virtual machine.

This is not to be confused with the VMDK descriptor file that is stored in the VM home namespace. The policy for snapshot delta files is inherited from the parent disks' policy. If there is none defined, the default policy of value for **Failures to Tolerate (FTT)** is set to 1.

Components

We discussed various object types and the fact that objects are distributed and stored across the hosts in the cluster; these distributed chunks of objects are called components. The components exist physically in the magnetic disk with a fair share of cache/buffer space from the flash device. Based on the stripe and mirroring requirements, the components are replicated and placed across the cluster.

The components are positioned in such a way that in the event of a host, network, or storage failure, and based on the policy associated, the object can be resurrected from the remaining available components from the available hosts in the cluster from an availability perspective. The stripe width will ensure that the relevant performance is serviced from the distributed components.

A witness

As with any split brain scenario, there is need for a reference point for the available node to declare and differentiate the failed node and take over the cluster responsibilities. In Virtual SAN, a similar concept applies. Assuming it's a RAID 1 scenario, there will be two copies/components for an object, and there will also be a witness component. In the event that the container (entire ESXi host's network failure or disk failure) of one of the components fails, the witness component serves as the reference point for the node that is still available.

Needless to say, the effectiveness of a witness will be dependent on the **Number of failures to tolerate** setting, which would ensure the necessary number of components available to sustain the failure threshold.

A witness purely plays a supporting role. As there is no actual data in the witness component, it comprises of metadata of about 2 MB just to serve the purpose.

Connecting the dots

Let's examine the physical layout and disk placement by connecting the dots between policies and objects, and between components and witnesses. Assume a virtual machine that has a single VMDK, A.vmdk. This vmdk file is the example of an object.

The object (A.vmdk) has been set with number of failures to tolerate as 1 and number of disk stripes as 2. This implies that there needs to be a mirrored copy of A.vmdk and VSAN should also split into two chunks to satisfy the stripe width requirement for performance enhancement. We have taken four ESXi hosts with two disk groups each to discuss the layout. It is important to note that this is one of the possible physical disk placements used by VSAN and not the only possibility.

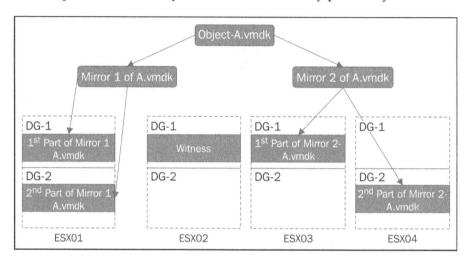

Consider the following steps:

- The A.vmdk file is first split into two mirrors to tolerate failure. As a rule of thumb, two mirrors cannot exist on the same host. This is to ensure that the object can tolerate a host failure.

- Each mirror is split into two components since the number of disk stripes per object is set to 2. With striping, however, all stripes may be collocated on the same host, since VSAN does not factor in the failure tolerance constraint while striping. The sole objective of striping is to have data spread across disk groups.

- Finally, we have a witness component to ensure acting as a reference point.

Internal building blocks of VSAN

Furthermore, there are internal components that work below the surface of VSAN. While an administrator may never have to deal with these components, a fair understanding of these components will help understand the internal workflow of VSAN and also to effectively troubleshoot issues.

We will discuss the following internal components of VSAN and how they work together:

- Reliable datagram transport
- Cluster monitoring, membership, and directory services
- Cluster-level object manager
- Distributed object manager
- Local log structured object manager

Reliable datagram transport

The primary backbone for VSAN functionality is the VMkernel port group for VSAN traffic and **reliable datagram transport** (**RDT**) operates on top of the VSAN VMkernel network to enable communication channels between the nodes participating in the VSAN cluster. RDT is optimized to transmit large chunks of data; it can set up and tear down transport connections based on underlying link status.

Cluster monitoring, membership, and directory services

The **cluster monitoring, membership, and directory services** (**CMMDS**) component is responsible for discovering, establishing, and maintaining the overall cluster health status.

The primary functions of CMMDS include:

- Managing an inventory of nodes, devices, and networks
- Maintaining policies, object metadata information, and configuration details
- Detecting failures in nodes and network paths, and updating RDT accordingly
- Maintaining a reusable directory service of information of disk, disk groups, and object information

Since CMMDS plays such a key role, there are roles introduced to handle failures effectively. CMMDS node plays the role of a master, backup, or agent. The master collates all the relevant information from the nodes and shares information as required back to the nodes. If a failure renders the CMMDS master in an inoperable state, the backup swiftly takes over the responsibility. The remaining nodes in the cluster play the agent role and only change roles if there is a failure of both master and backup nodes concurrently.

Cluster level object manager

Cluster level object manager (CLOM), as the name indicates, is the overall manager of objects at the cluster level. There is one CLOM instance on each node. It coordinates between all nodes to retrieve and maintain information pertaining to the number of nodes, disk groups, and disk space available across various disk groups. When an administrator attempts to create a virtual machine object, CLOM uses the information at its disposal to validate that there are sufficient resources to satisfy the object creation as per its policy.

CLOM can be thought of as the gatekeeper that allows or disallows object creation, and it also ensures compliance of an object to its set policies throughout its lifecycle.

The distributed object manager

The **distributed object manager (DOM)** provides distributed data access paths to objects. Once the CLOM validates that an object can be created, the DOM takes over and applies the configuration, that is, it deploys components locally through the help of LSOM. On completion of component creation locally, it communicates with its counterparts on other nodes in the cluster to deploy the remaining components on their respective disk groups.

All subsequent reads and writes to objects are funneled through the DOM that will take it to the appropriate component.

The local log structured object manager

The **local log structured object manager (LSOM)** operates at the lowest level and closely interfaces with the magnetic and flash devices. It provides the requisite physical persistent placement of virtual machine storage objects and also takes care of error retry and object recovery. Consider the following diagram:

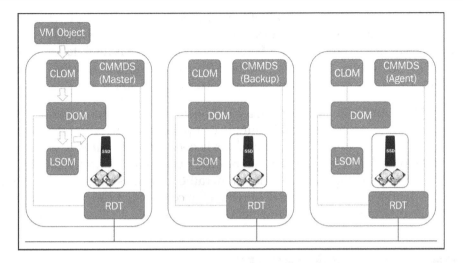

The preceding block diagram outlines the structure of the internal components of VSAN. This is the workflow through which CLOM validates resource availability and DOM creates components and applies configuration locally through LSOM and coordinates with counterparts for component creation on other nodes.

VSAN and high availability

A very crucial aspect of any product or solution is how it is able to sustain failure. With a VSAN infrastructure, this becomes all the more critical, since failure with its components may lead to data unavailability or data loss.

VSAN and **high availability (HA)** are interoperable thus far with vSphere, high availability was concerned with virtual machine availability. With the introduction of VSAN into the equation things are slightly different. In short, vSphere HA with VSAN is object centric. Here, we will assess the key components that make up VSAN, their failure scenarios, and how availability is ensured.

Primary components that attribute to availability are as follows:

- Magnetic disks
- Flash devices
- Host/network related failures

The key thing to remember is that all of the component failures are directly related to the **Number of failures to tolerate** setting. As long as the actual number of failures is lower than the configured failure threshold, there is no data loss or data unavailability. However, depending on the nature of the failure, whether transient or permanent, there may be a performance hit/overhead.

VSAN is able to intelligently tell when a component has failed permanently based on sense codes and will immediately initiate component regeneration that was associated to the component; this failure state is deemed as *degraded*. If VSAN cannot ascertain the nature of failure, which can be either transient or permanent, it does not immediately spawn component regeneration, rather classifies the state as "absent" and allows a threshold of 60 minutes in which the component can resume operation. After the cut-off time, component regeneration is initiated.

A magnetic disk failure

A magnetic disk of the disk group is the final resting place of data. The source of I/O to magnetic disk is when:

- Data written to flash is sequentially moved to magnetic disk (writes)
- Flash device is unable to service a READ (cache miss)
- In the backend, I/O is generated as part of a maintenance task to ensure compliance to policies (resync, replication, or data migration)

When there is a failure on the magnetic disk, the preceding tasks get impacted and the availability and access to data in the event of such a failure is dependent on the **Number of failure to tolerate** setting. By default, one failure can be sustained; in other words, the object/data residing on the failed disk has to be available elsewhere. If there is a read I/O targeted as the magnetic disk fails, the I/O is intercepted at the VSAN layer, which then redirects the read I/O to other replicas. In the event that no other replica exists, the I/O error is reported back to the virtual machine.

The write failures to the magnetic disk are reported back to the VSAN layer; this triggers a component regeneration.

In essence, if the tolerance level is sufficiently set to tolerate the failure, magnetic disk failure is fairly minor. The virtual machine continues to run even when the disk group that the magnetic disk was a part of continues to operate. This is demonstrated in the following diagram:

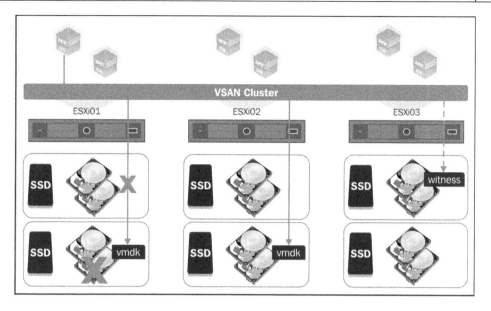

In the preceding example, assume the virtual machine is configured with failure to tolerate as 1. One of the magnetic disks in the disk group that happened to hold a component of the object has failed. The I/O that is directed towards this failed component is then redirected to its counterpart.

The other disks and disk groups in the cluster continue to operate as usual.

A flash device failure

Flash device failure has a relatively wider significance. This is because the flash device is the single point of failure for a disk group. Absence of an entire disk group implies that more components are likely to be impacted. All I/Os intended to this disk group are now redirected to other disk groups where replicas of the components exist.

From the performance perspective, reads that were serviced from the *active* dataset in the flash device, will now actually need to be fetched from the magnetic disk, and it is almost certain that there will be a relative increase in read latency.

A host failure

A host failure in a VSAN cluster effectively means that the disk groups from the specific host are unavailable and marked as "absent". This is because we are uncertain of the nature of the failure. From the perspective of data availability, a virtual machine that is running will continue to do so and the failure is transparent. As a rule of thumb, the components of an object are deployed in a fashion that would ensure it can sustain the failure threshold. In other words, the remaining hosts in the cluster will hold at least one other copy of the failed components that are absent due to the failed host.

VSAN also initiates the 60 minute timer. If the host returns within this threshold, the components resync with their counterparts to ensure that there is no delta. Beyond 60 minutes, component regeneration is initiated. The failed host may still return to the cluster, in which case, VSAN decides whether to pursue component regeneration or delta resync with the returned host. As a side effect of this, there may be orphaned, out-of-date, or partial data left over in VSAN. This is eventually removed and space is reclaimed.

Of course, the obvious question is: what happens to the virtual machines that were running on the failed host? This is dealt with in the same fashion as how conventional HA works in vSphere. The virtual machines are restarted on other hosts in the cluster while VSAN ensures object availability.

On a general note, when the host where the virtual machine is currently running fails, it will restart on a host that has access to more than 50 percent of the object, both in terms of network partition as well as isolation. This logic will ensure data availability to the VM.

Summary

We discussed the overall architecture and I/O flow on a VSAN datastore, the structure and components that enable such an architecture and facilitates performance, availability, and capacity management at the software layer. While most of the discussions are purely to understand how things work, there is very little that a vSphere administrator needs to worry about other than configuring the appropriate policies and letting VSAN do its magic.

In the next chapter, we will discuss some design considerations to optimize the VSAN design and adhere to certain best practices.

7
Design Considerations and Guidelines

In this chapter, we will discuss some of the design considerations and best practices for not required here VSAN. We will particularly look at fine tuning configuration parameters that will help yield optimal performance and availability.

Before we get into the details, it is important to remember that there are generally minimum requirements established by vendors for a product to be installed and configured. However, these minimum requirements are defined to ensure that there are sufficient resources to make the product work. In order to extract the best out of a product or solution, there is a strong likelihood that there is significant deviation from the minimum requirements and additional resources to build out an optimal design. This chapter will aim at looking at the nitty-gritty of configuration that is either internal or external to vSphere to aid in building such a design.

We will closely examine the following optimizations that play a key role in designing a VSAN cluster:

- Network optimizations
- Storage optimizations

Network optimizations

VSAN requires a VMkernel interface with the Virtual SAN traffic activated through which the cluster nodes communicate with each other. VSAN traffic comprises of a minimal amount of cluster-related administrative traffic and a large chunk of traffic that is attributed to object-related I/O.

From an IOPS perspective, if a specific block that is read or written to is not available on the local disk group, the I/O will need to traverse the VSAN network to other hosts that hold the referenced block. Furthermore, in the backend, to satisfy the availability requirements, data is being replicated. For instance, if there is a nonrecoverable physical disk failure, the objects residing on the specific disk are likely to have varying tolerance levels. Hence, the components existing on that physical device will be replicated through the VSAN network to make the objects associated with the virtual machine compliant with the policy set.

Hence, it is imperative to provide a stable, redundant, and sufficient throughput for VSAN network to operate. Physical and virtual network paths should be redundant and designed to eliminate single points of failure. Virtual SAN does not support multiple VMkernel adapters on the same subnet, unlike the multi-NIC vMotion feature that was introduced in vSphere 5. In addition, NIC teaming features provide the necessary availability; however, they do not provide load balancing capabilities. There are other means to load balance the cumulative traffic through design.

Outlined here are the parameters that play a key role in meeting the networking objectives for VSAN:

- MTU size
- Speed of the network interface
- Network I/O control

Jumbo frames

Jumbo frame is a generic networking concept wherein an Ethernet frame can be configured to carry 9000 bytes payload. By doing so, we reduce the CPU utilization and increase throughput. In the context of VSAN, there have been reports of performance improvement with jumbo frames enabled. The following VMware KB also outlines that jumbo frames should be enabled for best performance:

```
http://kb.vmware.com/kb/2058424
```

To enable jumbo frames on **vNetwork Distributed vSwitch (vDS)**, perform the following steps:

1. Login to the vSphere web client.
2. Traverse to **Home | Networking**.
3. Click on the respective vDS.
4. Traverse to **Manage | Properties**.

5. Now, navigate to **Edit | Advanced**.

6. Modify **MTU** to 9000.

The following screenshot shows the steps to set VSAN:

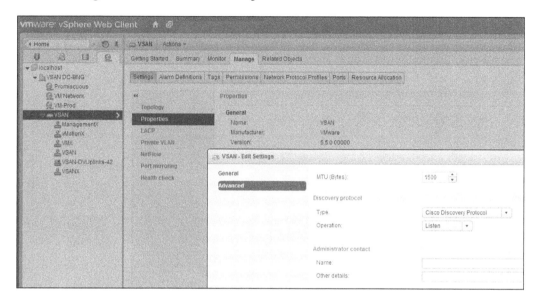

Speed of the network interface

The minimum requirement is to have a 1 GbE dedicated port for VSAN network from each host. It is highly recommended to have 10 GbE, as clearly outlined in VMware documentation, to satisfy the throughput and bandwidth requirements.

Network IO control

Network IO control (**NIOC**) is a feature of VDS. Any vSphere edition with Virtual SAN allows for vDS features to be used without any additional licenses. This by itself is a clear indication and recommendation to leverage NIOC with VSAN. To modify NIOC configuration settings, traverse to **Home | Networking** from the vSphere web client and select the respective VDS, as illustrated in the following screenshot:

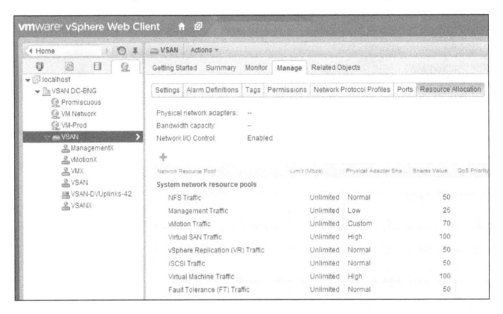

Isolation, shares, and limits

Primarily, NIOC aids in partitioning network capacity during contention. In addition, it also provides a good level of control over the usage of network bandwidth through isolation, shares, and limits. This will be particularly handy while sharing different traffic types on fewer uplinks. With the advent of 10 GbE and converged network adapters, such configuration has become a more common requirement for better control at the software level and QoS implementation.

From a vSphere networking perspective, we will need to facilitate the following network traffic:

- Management network (vmk0)
- vMotion network (vmk1)
- Virtual machine network
- VSAN network (vmk2)

We will need to ensure that sufficient bandwidth is allocated to the port groups while redundancy is factored. Given that, our recommendations are inclined toward 10 GbE. We can facilitate the requirements with 1 x 10 GbE and can add another network card for purposes of redundancy.

Furthermore, as opposed to setting a limit on the bandwidth consumed by the various traffic types, we will set shares for the traffic types. The effect of shares will kick in only during congestion: the available bandwidth will be proportionally allocated to the traffic type based on the shares allocated. By default, a system network resource pool exists with all traffic types allocated 50 shares, albeit virtual machine traffic that gets 100 shares.

We do not anticipate congestion in a 2 x 10 GbE network configuration. However, on a precautionary note, proportionally increasing the shares of Virtual SAN traffic over other traffic will ensure that it gets higher prioritization.

Note that any noncontributing traffic type on the resource pool will not affect the bandwidth distribution.

Let's walk through this with a sample design.

Assume the following distribution of shares:

Traffic type	Physical adapter shares
Management	20
vMotion	50
Virtual machine network	30
VSAN	100

Based on our requirements outlined earlier, a distributed switch can be created as follows:

1. Create a VDS with 2 x 10 GbE uplink interfaces.
2. Dedicate a 1 X 10 GbE NIC (vmnic0) for VSAN network port group.
3. Set vmnic1 as a standby for VSAN network port group.
4. Share management, vMotion, and virtual machine on the other 1 x 10 GbE NIC (vmnic1).
5. Set vmnic0 as a standby adapter for management, vMotion, and virtual machine.

The physical network layout will appear as follows:

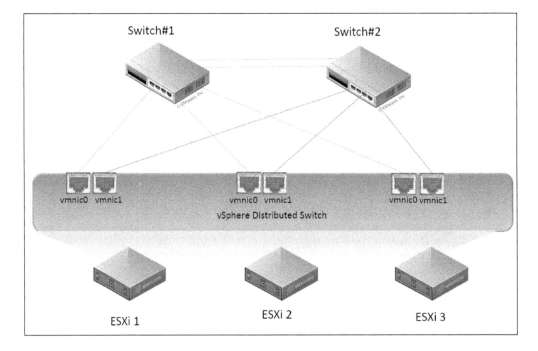

The following is the vSphere Distributed Switch configuration:

Traffic type	Teaming option	Active uplink	Standby uplink
Management	Explicit failover	vmnic1	vmnic0
vMotion	Explicit failover	vmnic1	vmnic0
VSAN	Explicit failover	vmnic0	vmnic1
Virtual machine	Explicit failover	vmnic1	vmnic0

Under normal operating conditions, the traffic is naturally segregated with VSAN traffic getting a dedicated 10 GbE network card, as per best practices. For the other traffic types, there is more than sufficient bandwidth available with a complete 10 GbE network card considering that these traffic types each commonly get 1 x 1 GbE or 2 x 1 GbE NICs.

In the event that there is a failure of one of the NICs and simultaneously active traffic is generated from VSAN, vMotion, virtual machine, and management networks, it may lead to congestion. At this juncture, the shares configured will kick in and prioritize traffic based on its criticality, that is, when we have only one 10 GbE NIC operational. The following table outlines the best case and worst case scenarios:

Traffic type	Shares	Guaranteed bandwidth allocation 2 x 10 GbE	Guaranteed bandwidth allocation 1 x 10 GbE (1 NIC failure)
Management	20	2 GBps	1 GBps
vMotion	50	5 GBps	2.5 GBps
Virtual machine network	30	3 GBps	1.5 GBps
VSAN	100	10 GBps	5 GBps

Note that the virtual machine network traffic requirements are specific to environments and may need to be provided higher prioritization.

Similarly, other teaming policies can be adapted with the exception of a route based on IP hash. IP hash has additional constraints that are explained in the VMware KB article available at `http://kb.vmware.com/kb/2006129`. Furthermore, VMware documentation clearly outlines that IP hash does not guarantee any performance improvements.

Quality of Service

Quality of Service (QoS) on traffic types provides an additional layer of guarantee of traffic prioritization. This is, however, only an extension of the common network concept, that is, to the vSphere networking.

It specifies a priority value between 0 and 7 (inclusive) that can be used by QoS disciplines to differentiate traffic. This technique is commonly referred to as IEEE 802.1p. There is no standard or amendment by this name published by IEEE. Rather, the technique is incorporated into the IEEE 802.1Q standard, which specifies the tag inserted into an Ethernet frame.

IEEE recommendations on the traffic classification are outlined here:

Priority	Acronym	Traffic types
0 (lowest)	BK	Background
1	BE	Best effort
2	EE	Excellent effort
3	CA	Critical applications
4	VI	Video less than 100 ms latency and jitter
5	VO	Voice less than 10 ms latency and jitter
6	IC	Internetwork control
7 (highest)	NC	Network control

To summarize, from a network perspective, jumbo frames, network card speed, and NIOC work in conjunction to deliver optimal VSAN performance. In addition, we require properly configured upstream network equipment to guarantee stable and reliable multicast performance to support VSAN infrastructure.

Storage configuration optimizations

We will assess storage configuration optimizations with each of the physical hardware components that make up the VSAN and their interdependency.

A flash device

Based on the discussion so far, we know that the first point of contact on disk for any I/O is the flash device. Therefore, the **Performance Class** SSD, as defined by the respective vendors and by **VMware Compatibility Guide (VCG)**, is an important factor in the design consideration. From a design point of view, the VSAN sizing tool (http://virtualsansizing.vmware.com/) helps to choose the right combination of quality and quantity to deliver estimated IOPS from the cluster.

Alternatively, you can specifically check the IOPS capability through VCG. The following screenshot from the VCG highlights the performance class for the supported makes and models of SSD:

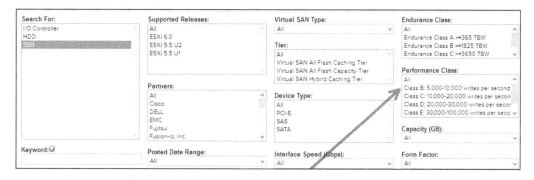

Magnetic disks

Magnetics disks come into play during data destage for write and read cache miss. To ensure that bottlenecks don't develop during these stages, an appropriate RPM and interface speed of the magnetic disks are to be factored in during the design.

I/O controllers

VSAN funnels I/O through the controller to the respective disks attached. Hence, the controller can be quite an impediment to performance. The key parameter that governs the efficiency of the I/O controller is the queue depth and the minimum requirement for any I/O controller to support VSAN is 256. The optimal queue depth should suffice to accommodate the cumulative queue depth (or higher) of all the disks attached.

Cache-to-capacity ratio

Virtual SAN's object-based storage model and the policies naturally provide the ability to ensure that data is stored in a distributed fashion, and a flash device proportionally allows for read/write IOPS enhancement. To optimize this further in both aspects of performance and availability, we need to relook at the disk group composition, that is, the cache-to-capacity ratio.

Let's revisit the supported limits of VSAN datastore composition.

Note that in VSAN 6.0 the limits are unchanged, however, all-flash support is introduced. More details on these lines are discussed in *Chapter 9, What's New in VSAN 6.0?*. The following table outlines the supported limits of VSAN datastore composition:

Item	Maximum
Disk groups per host	5
Magnetic disk per disk groups	7
SSD disks per disk group	1

Although there are several permutations and combinations of the disk group composition and number of disk groups, the underlying factors that influence the optimal design are subjective to the nature of the workloads.

The starting point to designing a VSAN cluster is to ascertain the estimated cumulative capacity that is required inclusive of storage capacity required by the virtual machine to be hosted in the cluster along with the level of redundancy for the data. This leads the way to the overall cluster size and capacity required per host.

At this juncture, you need to define the number of flash devices and capacity of each flash device. These two factors have a very high influence on the performance of a VSAN cluster.

Capacity

A vSphere administrator may develop a perception that capacity consumption of virtual machines on VSAN storage is rather high, that is, virtual machine objects have a default FTT set to 1, and so the consumed capacity is twice as much. It must be understood that VSAN implements RAID at the software layer and is no different to how capacity is consumed from disks backing a LUN that is configured as RAID 1.

With VSAN, we know that the capacity tier is rather cheap. Yet by design, the default policy deploys thin provisioned VMDKs. Nonetheless, from a capacity planning perspective, the overall sizing of the VSAN datastore should factor in the FTT that is set to objects and capacity tier should be sized sufficiently to accommodate all the virtual machine objects including the mirrors.

Performance

Flash device usage in VSAN has a ratio of 30:70 for write buffer and read cache. The recommended sizing of the flash capacity for Virtual SAN is to use 10 percent of the anticipated consumed storage capacity before the number of failures to tolerate is considered.

This statement needs a bit more clarity, so let's understand this with an example. Assume that you have one large VM with VMDK of size 100 GB with the policy for FTT set to 1 on a VSAN datastore. This implies that the VMDK object will have two components, one of which is a mirrored copy (component).

Therefore, the total consumed space of the object before FTT is considered is 100 GB and the total consumed space of the object after FTT is considered is 200 GB. To compute the flash capacity, we should consider the former, that is, the recommended size (which in this scenario is 10 GB of flash). In a real-world scenario, an administrator should factor-in some buffer capacity for metadata and swap file size cumulative of all virtual machines that would be placed in the VSAN datastore to deduce the required flash capacity.

Overall, this recommendation should suffice in most cases. Theoretically, we know that all writes and most reads hit the flash. In situations where the amount of flash does not suffice, which depend on your specific workloads, additional flash disk capacity may be needed. In the next chapter, we will discuss the ways to identify issues whereby IOPS overflow the provisioned flash capacity.

It is expected that careful design considerations are made based on the workloads with the sizing. Some generic guidelines based on the workload types can be referenced from the guide for VSAN ready nodes available at `http://partnerweb. vmware.com/programs/vsan/Virtual%20SAN%20Ready%20Nodes.pdf`.

Availability

In a failure scenario in the context of disk, there could be potentially a magnetic disk failure or a flash device failure. Both have varying degrees of impact. Assume that a magnetic disk fails on a specific disk group. There may be I/O referencing to the components that resided in the physical disks and these need to be fetched from another replica of the failed components, provided the default FTT is at least 1. On the contrary, an SSD failure has a bigger impact, causing a complete disk group to be nonfunctional. This is the second dimension of disk group composition, that is, the SSD becomes a single point of failure of the disk group. This is because the maximum number of SSDs per disk group is one, and can be easily mitigated by distributing the flash capacity to multiple SSDs and therefore multiple disk groups. In other words, instead of one large disk group, you can have two smaller disk groups.

A scale-out design

To answer a common question on the influence of Virtual SAN on consolidation ratio and cluster sizing, it only adds a layer of complexity in terms of coupling disk capacity with compute capacity, which otherwise are two mutually exclusive requirements.

By nature of Virtual SAN architecture, it accommodates cluster growth in terms of storage capacity, or compute, or both. In essence, the cluster size needs to be in the VSAN range of minimum to maximum nodes supported, of which only three of the hosts need to contribute to the VSAN datastore. So, in reality, depending on the resource utilization and bottleneck, an administrator can incrementally add disk or compute to scale out.

The number of hosts per cluster and VM to host ratio does not deviate from the traditional design and sizing mechanisms adapted in a virtualized infrastructure. However, there is an additional section in configuration maximums for vSphere 5.x and 6.x guides published by VMware that now includes maximums with VSAN.

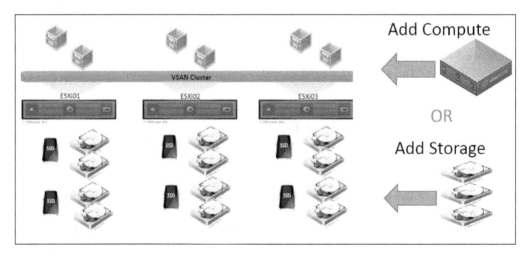

Backing up your VSAN workloads

By setting FTT, there is a natural failure tolerance that VSAN offers and a copy of the object suffices for the virtual machine data to be available and accessible. However, it is not a replacement for having a backup. There are a several ways to design backup solutions for VSAN-backed VMs. While it is not in the scope of this book to go into configuration details of the backup utilities, we will discuss some common mechanisms that are natively available with VMware products:

- Create a local backup to VSAN through **vSphere Data Protection (VDP)**
- Create a local backup to VMFS/NFS through VDP
- Create a remote backup through VDP
- vSphere replication

Note that, with effect from March 1, 2015, VMware vSphere Data Protection Advanced will be consolidated into VMware vSphere Data Protection. All functionalities have been merged in VMware vSphere Data Protection. Earlier, this product was delivered as standalone and required a separate license.

Creating a local backup through VDP

This is perhaps the most straightforward backup design for VSAN. A VDP appliance is deployed on the same VSAN cluster of the target VM that ought to be backed up. You do not need twice the capacity for appliance, as it can effectively "deduplicate" the content. While experimenting with the samples of workload of varied natures/platforms, VDP can deduplicate 1 TB of data to less than 100 GB. The following diagram provides an overview of this backup design:

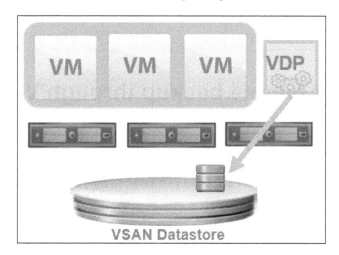

As the diagram illustrates, a compressed VDP repository backs up data and stores it back on the same VSAN datastore. This is a fairly simple design that will effectively mitigate loss of a VM that was not sufficiently protected by FTT and solve most examples for backup. The rule of thumb with backup, however, is not to keep your backup data in the same storage repository of production data. A catastrophic failure to the entire VSAN datastore will lead to complete data loss, leaving VDP ineffective.

Creating a local backup to VMFS/NFS through VDP

In line with standard recommendations, the backup repository can be moved to alternate storage by presenting a VMFS or NFS datastore to the cluster. This will yield an architecture as illustrated here:

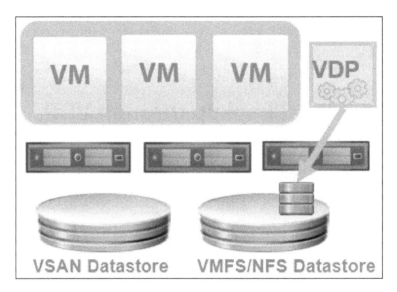

Creating a remote backup through VDP

To mitigate site-level failure, the VDP feature to replicate backup data can be used to build a redundant VDP appliance on a remote site. This makes it possible to back up data locally and then replicate this backup data to another VDP advanced appliance. The resulting design is illustrated in the following diagram:

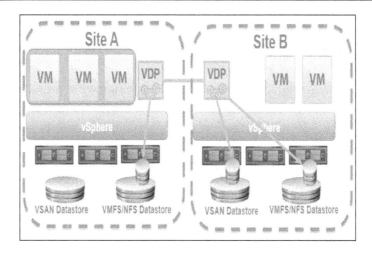

vSphere Replication to protect VSAN

vSphere Replication (**VR**) is a host-based replication solution and is independent of the storage backing the vSphere infrastructure. VR can replicate between heterogeneous storage, that is, SAN to VSAN, NAS, DAS, or vice-versa. Hence, another feasible design to sustain site-level failures is to integrate the replication through vSphere Replication. VR manages replication from protection site to replication site and VSAN can be leveraged at either end. This is to state that VSAN can be used purely as a DR site storage solution as well.

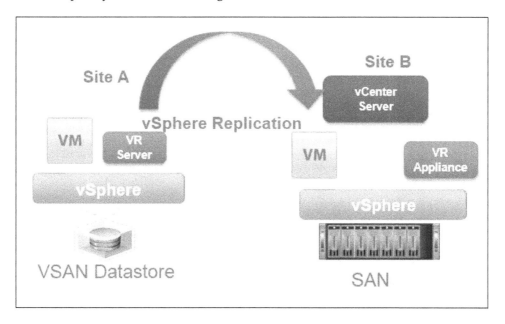

The following are the key points to remember while using VDP:

- A VDP appliance would greatly benefit with the maximum number of stripes from a performance standpoint
- Restoring or overwriting to the original VM retains the previous storage policy
- Restoring to a newer location causes the default policy to be applied
- While VDP ensures judicious use of capacity through deduplication, to further optimize capacity consumption you may reduce the FTT from 1 to 0 while the VDP appliance replicates to another VDP appliance

Summary

In conclusion, it is fairly easy to set up a VSAN cluster. A carefully thought out design helps to take it to the next level and to get the best out of VSAN. At a granular level, getting the right composition of disk groups catering to the workload type is of utmost importance, followed by infrastructure-level optimizations. Disaster recovery and backup solutions aim to provide additional resiliency and mitigate any catastrophic failures that may occur.

In the next chapter, we will closely assess the utilities that would aid in closer introspection of the VSAN infrastructure for sustained monitoring and enhancements catering to the specific workloads.

8
Troubleshooting and Monitoring Utilities for Virtual SAN

In this chapter, we will discuss troubleshooting by leveraging various utilities to diagnose common problems that can surface in a Virtual SAN environment. The primary focus is on retrieving information that is not readily available on the GUI, delving into statistical data to ensure the desired level of performance, and eliminating anomalies at a very early stage.

The overall objective of this chapter is to proactively monitor the VSAN infrastructure and familiarize with tools to expedite the troubleshooting process by chasing down the components that are exhibiting abnormal behavior. We will discuss the following topics:

- Troubleshooting workflow
- Understanding the software components of VSAN
- ESXCLI namespace (based on the command line)
- Ruby vSphere Console (based on the command line)
- VSAN Observer (based on the graphical user interface)

Troubleshooting workflow

Building a VSAN cluster is fairly straightforward with just enabling a checkbox, in a similar way to HA/DRS. The underlying design and interaction, however, is fairly complex. Hence, troubleshooting an issue can be quite cumbersome.

It is recommended to adopt a modular or step-by-step approach when troubleshooting a VSAN issue.

Validating the hardware and configuration limit

As a rule of thumb, the starting point of any investigation is validating that the platform backend is designed, certified, and tested for the solution that is implemented.

VSAN is particularly sensitive in this aspect. Hence, the primary validation before troubleshooting an issue is to ensure that all the components of Virtual SAN are supported and certified in line with the latest VMware HCL.

Also, this has been the primary cause for most of the issues with Virtual SAN that have been reported, and is more prone to environments that are built from scratch as opposed to deploying through VSAN - ready nodes or EVO: RAIL.

Following this, verify whether there have been any threshold/configuration limits that have been exceeded. Specific versions of the product comprise of configuration maximums guidelines. We can perform most of the validation through the vSphere UI and command-line utilities in this chapter.

We will follow the following workflow, in increasing order of complexity:

- Understanding the software components of VSAN
- ESXCLI namespace
- Ruby vSphere Console
- VSAN Observer

Understanding the software components of VSAN

Before getting started, let's revisit and look at some brief definitions of the key software components that make up Virtual SAN. An understanding of the roles aids in channeling troubleshooting efforts to the appropriate component.

The log structured object manager

The VSAN LSOM (log structured object manager) operates at the physical disk level. The role of the LSOM includes the physical placement of components into a disk group, storing configuration information and storage policy associated to objects, I/O retry on error conditions, SSD log recovery, and reporting events associated to the devices.

The distributed object manager

The DOM provides distributed data access paths to objects built from local (LSOM) components. The DOM is responsible for the creation of reliable, fault-tolerant VM storage objects from local components across multiple ESXi hosts in the VSAN cluster. DOM is also responsible for handling different types of failures, such as I/O failing from a device and unable to contact a host. In the event of an unexpected host failure during recovery, DOM must resynchronize all the components that make up every object. Components publish a `bytesToSync` value periodically to show the progress of a synchronize operation.

In essence, VSAN designates an "owner" for every storage object. The owner is responsible for coordinating the delivery of I/O to the intended object. The CLOM is responsible for ensuring compliance of an object to the associated storage policy. It can be thought of as the overall supervisory module that sends down instructions to the DOM that implements the instructions or puts them into action.

Cluster monitoring, membership, and directory services

CMMDS does exactly what its name implies; it monitors, maintains membership, and acts as directory.

The ESXCLI namespace

With the advent of VSAN, the ESXCLI namespace includes VSAN-specific commands. You may run into situations where hostd, the management agent running on the ESXi host, becomes unresponsive and you are unable to manage the host through UI-based tools. In such instances, the ESXCLI namespace does not function either. This is because ESXCLI is dependent on hostd.

In most circumstances, administrators resort to the command line only when the environment is unmanageable through the UI, and the inability to run ESXCLI can greatly hamper troubleshooting. In such cases, you can execute the localcli commands, which are equivalent to ESXCLI commands; however, it bypasses hostd and executes the command. Localcli should be reserved for times when ESXCLI does not respond in a timely fashion. If used, it is recommended that you restart hostd right afterwards, otherwise the system may get into an inconsistent state.

To obtain help with the syntax, usage, or the list of available commands, you can suffix the command with -h, as follows:

```
~ # esxcli vsan -h
```

Its usage is as follows:

```
esxcli vsan {cmd} [cmd options]
```

Here is the list of available namespaces:

Namespace	Description
datastore	This commands for VSAN datastore configuration
network	This commands for VSAN host network configuration
storage	This commands for VSAN physical storage configuration
cluster	This commands for VSAN host cluster configuration
maintenancemode	This commands for VSAN maintenance mode operation
policy	This commands for VSAN storage policy configuration
trace	This commands for VSAN trace configuration

Let's review and elaborate on the usage of these namespaces in commands.

Datastore

An administrator can view or change the VSAN datastore name using the datastore namespace. The information is set or obtained at the host level by logging in through SSH. There is hardly any use case for executing this command unless you are inclined to do things the UNIX way. Otherwise, this namespace is just a sophisticated way of performing a set/get task that can be easily performed through the vSphere web client.

Also, the set option modifies the datastore name at the host level. Either this needs to be consistently performed across all hosts or, preferably, the task needs to be performed from the vSphere web client.

The syntax to start datastore is:

```
~ # esxcli vsan datastore
```

It can be used as follows:

```
esxcli vsan datastore {cmd} [cmd options]
```

The available namespaces will be listed as follows:

```
  name                    Commands for configuring VSAN datastore name.
```

The other syntax for `datastore` is:

```
~ # esxcli vsan datastore name
```

Its usage is as follows:

```
esxcli vsan datastore name {cmd} [cmd options]
```

Here is the list of available commands:

Commands	Description
get	This gets the VSAN datastore name.
set	This configures the VSAN datastore name. In general, renaming should always be done at the cluster level. Across a VSAN, cluster, the VSAN datastore (SP1) name should be in sync.

Network

Network serves as the backbone for internode communication, and can potentially be prone to several issues. The following section discusses the useful commands for this namespace:

Its syntax is:

```
~ # esxcli vsan network
```

It can be used as follows:

```
esxcli vsan network {cmd} [cmd options]
```

The available namespaces are listed as follows:

```
  ipv4                    Commands for configuring IPv4 network for VSAN.
```

Here is the list of available commands:

Command	Description
clear	This clears the VSAN network configuration.
list	This lists the network configuration currently used by VSAN.
remove	This removes an interface from the VSAN network configuration.
restore	This restores the persisted VSAN network configuration.

The other syntax for `network` is:

```
~ # esxcli vsan network list
Interface
VmkNic Name: vmk1
    IP Protocol: IPv4
    Interface UUID: 529b6754-9b3a-a6d1-d6e3-74867aee0146
    Agent Group Multicast Address: 224.2.3.4
    Agent Group Multicast Port: 23451
    Master Group Multicast Address: 224.1.2.3
    Master Group Multicast Port: 12345
    Multicast TTL: 5
```

The preceding command reveals useful information about the VMkernel interface, where VSAN is configured, the IP protocol (IPv4) multicast details. The information comes in handy in situations where you suspect that network communication is causing issues, similar to the following screenshot:

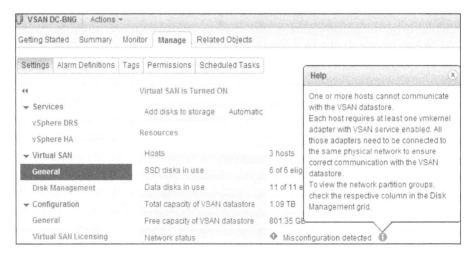

In addition to this, the standard ESXCLI network namespace inclusively provides all the network stack information that can be used in troubleshooting connectivity and packet capture.

Storage

The `esxcli vsan storage` namespace is a powerful tool to manipulate a disk group set up in VSAN. A good level of understanding and expertise is recommended when executing these commands.

Its syntax is:

```
~ # esxcli vsan storage
```

It can be used as follows:

```
esxcli vsan storage {cmd} [cmd options]
```

The available namespaces are listed as follows:

```
   automode               Commands for configuring VSAN storage auto claim
mode.
```

Here is the list of available commands:

Command	Description
add	This adds physical disk for the VSAN usage
list	This lists the VSAN storage configuration
remove	This removes physical disks from the VSAN disk groups

The `automode` namespace is Boolean in nature, so you can ascertain whether the mode is automatic or manual, and also toggle the settings:

```
~ # esxcli vsan storage automode get
Enabled: true
```

You can also list/add/remove physical disks from a disk group with the relevant commands:

```
~ # esxcli vsan storage list
naa.5001e820026cfa60
   Device: naa.5001e820026cfa60
   Display Name: naa.5001e820026cfa60
   Is SSD: true
```

```
    VSAN UUID: 52483341-9e91-772a-7fcd-f8636c6a187e

    VSAN Disk Group UUID: 52483341-9e91-772a-7fcd-f8636c6a187e

    VSAN Disk Group Name: naa.5001e820026cfa60

    Used by this host: true

    In CMMDS: true

    Checksum: 6502489929502758938

    Checksum OK: true


naa.5000c5006bc133d7

    Device: naa.5000c5006bc133d7

    Display Name: naa.5000c5006bc133d7

    Is SSD: false

    VSAN UUID: 5223e52b-5063-e870-8c99-f13ac9f689c7

    VSAN Disk Group UUID: 52483341-9e91-772a-7fcd-f8636c6a187e

    VSAN Disk Group Name: naa.5001e820026cfa60

    Used by this host: true

    In CMMDS: true

    Checksum: 12097475659803588221

    Checksum OK: true


naa.5000c5006bc03273

    Device: naa.5000c5006bc03273

    Display Name: naa.5000c5006bc03273

    Is SSD: false

    VSAN UUID: 52352867-2c80-e84b-c2ce-812a5c0a9b76

    VSAN Disk Group UUID: 52483341-9e91-772a-7fcd-f8636c6a187e

    VSAN Disk Group Name: naa.5001e820026cfa60

    Used by this host: true

    In CMMDS: true

    Checksum: 12971806586651341606

    Checksum OK: true
```

There are several identifiers to distinguish one disk group from another. One very useful identifier is VSAN Disk Group Name. As seen in the preceding example, VSAN Disk Group Name is naa.5001e820026cfa60, which is the actual NAA ID of the SSD disk in the group. This should effectively help to ascertain the number of disk groups and the composition of each disk group. The Is SSD boolean flag denotes whether the specific disk is SSD or not.

The Used by this host identifier denotes whether the specific disk is claimed by the host. As you can imagine, this can provide useful insights for troubleshooting issues surrounding disk unavailability, capacity-related issues, and much more.

The In CMMDS identifier is indicative of cluster monitoring, membership, and directory service status. While true reflects a healthy state, if the flag is set to false, it indicates that the specific disk(s) no longer contribute to the disk group capacity. If their cumulative capacity does not add up, or if there are discrepancies, this command would provide the correct directive.

While esxcli vsan storage list is non-intrusive and read-only, the other commands such as add and remove have an impact on the disk composition and performance. The add command is obviously used when the disk group's automode option is set to false, and to effectively add a new SSD or magnetic disk. This is a classic use case when you need to scale out. The administrator moves the host to the maintenance mode, adds physical disks to the server, and subsequently adds the disk through this command.

The opposite of this is to remove an SSD or a magnetic disk from the group. Needless to say, this command should be executed with caution, as this option removes all the data from the indicated disk.

VSAN expects an empty disk with no partitions, in cases where partitions are present, the disk has to be partitioned and formatted, otherwise this operation will fail. The command expects the device name for the disk to be provided, for instance mpx.vmhba2:C0:T1:L0. SSDs are added with the -s|--ssd switch and magnetic disks are used with the -d|--disk switch, respectively.

For removal, you can also mention the UUID of the VSAN disk instead of the `-s|--ssd` or `-d|--disk` switches. The steps to remove a device are demonstrated here:

1. Identify the NAA ID of the device to be removed by executing the command `vsan.disks_stats 0`:

```
/10.112.102.202/VSAN DC-BNG/computers>vsan.disks_stats 0
```

The output will be similar to this:

```
+----------------------+----------------+-------+------+-----------
+------+----------+--------+
|                      |                |       | Num  | Capacity
|      |          Status |
| DisplayName          | Host           | isSSD | Comp | Total
| Used | Reserved | Health |
+----------------------+----------------+-------+------+-----------
+------+----------+--------+
| naa.5001e820026cfa08 | 10.109.10.107  | SSD   | 0    | 260.83 GB
| 0 %  | 0 %      | OK     |
| naa.5000c5006bc133d7 | 10.109.10.107  | MD    | 0    | 279.25 GB
| 0 %  | 0 %      | OK     |
| naa.5000c5006bc22e17 | 10.109.10.107  | MD    | 0    | 279.25 GB
| 0 %  | 0 %      | OK     |
+----------------------+----------------+-------+------+-----------
+------+----------+--------+
```

2. Obtain the details of the NAA ID through the ESXCLI namespace executed against the host:

```
/10.112.102.202/VSAN DC-BNG/computers> esxcli 0/
hosts/10.109.10.107 storage nmp device list
```

The output will look similar to this:

```
Checksum: "4900938534405155606"

ChecksumOK: true

Device: "naa.5000c5006bc22e17"

DisplayName: "naa.5000c5006bc22e17"

InCMMDS: true

IsSSD: false

Usedbythishost: true

VSANDiskGroupName: "naa.5001e820026cfa08"

VSANDiskGroupUUID: "52c643f6-033c-caed-4494-c010fd6ff6a5"

VSANUUID: "526c5e80-8bf0-fedb-58f6-6bef96db1097"
```

3. Remove the device with the following command:

```
/10.112.102.202/VSAN DC-BNG/computers> esxcli 0/
hosts/10.109.10.107 vsan storage remove -u 526c5e80-8bf0-fedb-
58f6-6bef96db1097
```

4. Rerun `vsan.disks_stats` to ensure that the device is removed:

```
/10.112.102.202/VSAN DC-BNG/computers>vsan.disks_stats 0
```

The output will now look like this:

```
+--------------------+--------------+------+-----+----------
+------+---------+--------+
|                    |              |      | Num | Capacity
|          | Status |
| DisplayName| Host |isSSD | Comp | Total| Used | Reserved |
Health |
+--------------------+--------------+------+-----+----------
+-+
|naa.5001e820026cfa08 |10.109.10.107|SSD|0| 260.83 GB | 0 %  | 0
%        | OK|
| naa.5000c5006bc133d7|10.109.10.107 |MD|0| 279.25 GB | 0 %  | 0
%        | OK|
+--------------------+--------------+------+-----+----------
+------+---------+--------+
```

Cluster

Consider a scenario where you have three physical hosts in the data center that are newly procured and you intend to deploy the VSAN solution. Here we have a catch-22 situation, to deploy vCenter we need a storage repository (VSAN), to create the storage repository we need vCenter. One of the options to counter this is to bootstrap VSAN without vCenter. To achieve this, we depend heavily on the ESXCLI namespace. This process is outlined more precisely at http://www.vmware.com/files/pdf/products/vsan/VMware-TechNote-Bootstrapping-VSAN-without-vCenter.pdf.

In this section, we will discuss the significance of the cluster-related commands.

Its syntax is:

```
~ # esxcli vsan cluster
```

It can be used as follows:

```
esxcli vsan cluster {cmd} [cmd options]
```

Here is the list of the available commands:

Commands	Description
get	This gets the information of the VSAN cluster that this host is joined to.
join	This joins the host to a given VSAN cluster.
leave	This leaves the VSAN cluster that the host is currently joined to.
restore	This restores the persisted VSAN cluster configuration.

To obtain cluster information, we execute the `get` command:

```
~ # esxcli vsan cluster get
Cluster Information
   Enabled: true
   Current Local Time: 2015-01-18T07:26:29Z
   Local Node UUID: 536a162d-2ab1-116e-d910-74867aee01ca
   Local Node State: BACKUP
   Local Node Health State: HEALTHY
   Sub-Cluster Master UUID: 536a20d1-60d3-ab9d-3206-74867aee0146
   Sub-Cluster Backup UUID: 536a162d-2ab1-116e-d910-74867aee01ca
   Sub-Cluster UUID: 526a4992-690a-4ca5-3bc9-6c7f056d7fd1
   Sub-Cluster Membership Entry Revision: 3
   Sub-Cluster Member UUIDs: 536a162d-2ab1-116e-d910-74867aee01ca,
536a20d1-60d3-ab9d-3206-74867aee0146, 536a5c03-8268-4a67-a3ef-
b8ca3af6a80e
   Sub-Cluster Membership UUID: b3847154-eec1-60d7-f5fa-74867aee0146
```

The key information we draw from the output is the node state—the node can be a master, backup, or an agent. We also get information about the specific node's UUID as well as the master and backup nodes' UUIDs. Member UUIDs should effectively display all the nodes participating in the VSAN cluster. Missing nodes indicate network connectivity issues.

Policy

Efficiency of VSAN lies mainly in its policy-based management. The `esxcli vsan policy` namespace allows a certain degree of management of the default policies. You can either clear, get, or set the default policies. Default policies are essentially failback policies to which objects are associated if there are no user-defined policies.

Its syntax is:

```
~ # esxcli vsan policy
```

It can be used as follows:

```
esxcli vsan policy {cmd} [cmd options]
```

Here is the list of available commands:

Commands	Description
cleardefault	This clears the default VSAN storage policy values.
getdefault	This gets the default VSAN storage policy values.
setdefault	This sets the default VSAN storage policy values.

To view the default policies set, we run the `getdefault` command:

```
~ # esxcli vsan policy getdefault
Policy Class   Policy Value
-----------    ---------------------------------------------------------
cluster        (("hostFailuresToTolerate" i1))
vdisk          (("hostFailuresToTolerate" i1))
vmnamespace    (("hostFailuresToTolerate" i1))
vmswap         (("hostFailuresToTolerate" i1) ("forceProvisioning" i1))
```

Policies are segregated for each type of object, and by default, all the objects can tolerate one failure:

Policy Class	Object Type
vdisk	VMDK and snapshot delta
vmnamespace	The VM home namespace
vmswap	Swap
cluster	Catch all

There may be situations where you need to modify the default set policies. You can leverage the five modify policy settings associated with VSAN; the settings are discussed at length in *Chapter 4, Getting Started with VSAN – Installation and Configuration*.

The syntax is as follows:

```
esxclivsan policy "-p|--policy=<str>" "-c|--policy-class=<str>"
cacheReservation
forceProvisioning
hostFailuresToTolerate
stripeWidth
proportionalCapacity
```

Other useful namespaces

ESXCLI has two additional namespaces that are seldom used and we will also look at two additional utilities that may be helpful in some corner cases.

esxcli vsan maintenancemode

The maintenance mode namespace only allows an administrator to cancel a maintenance mode operation that is in progress:

```
~ # esxcli vsan maintenancemode
```

It can be used as follows:

```
esxcli vsanmaintenancemode {cmd} [cmd options]
```

Here is the list of available commands:

Commands	Description
cancel	This cancels a VSAN maintenance mode operation which is in progress

esxcli vsan trace

The `esxcli vsan trace` namespace is a troubleshooting and diagnostic utility. It is particularly useful for advanced troubleshooting and gathering detailed information. This information may be requested by VMware to diagnose certain issues, along with instructions on the number of files and size.

Its syntax is:

```
~ # esxcli vsan trace set -h
```

It can be used as follows:

```
esxcli vsan trace set [cmd options]
```

The set command is available with this namespace, which is used to configure VSAN trace. Note that this command is not thread safe.

Here is the list of available command options:

- -f|--numfiles=<long>: This logs file rotation for VSAN trace files.
- -p|--path=<str>: This is the path to store VSAN trace files.
- -r|--reset: When set to true, this resets defaults for VSAN trace files.
- -s|--size=<long>: This displays the maximum size of VSAN trace files in MB.

cmmds-tool

The cmmds-tool command provides some additional insight, and more specifically, can help obtain data-related information. Earlier, we saw that the ESXCLI namespace could bootstrap VSAN without vCenter and, in general, how VSAN could be maintained and managed without vCenter. The cmmds-tool command moves this up a notch higher and can be used to perform certain advanced tasks without the vCenter. This is only informational and for awareness, and it should be used under the guidance and supervision of VMware technical support.

The help menu can be retrieved through the -h|--help switch:

```
~ # cmmds-tool -h
usage: cmmds-tool <cmd> <options>
commands:
    add                     Adds an entry from stdin. On successful exit the
                            entry is guaranteed to be in the directory
    delete                  Deletes matching entries. On successful exit the
                            entry will be deleted from the directory
    dump                    Dumps first matching entry to stdout
    find                    Finds matching entries
    wait                    Waits for a matching entry to appear
    waitdump                Waits for a matching entry to appear and dumps
                            the entry to stdout
    waitformembership       Waits for a membership entry to appear
    whoami                  Get the node's uuid as used in the sub-cluster
    amimember               Check if I am the member in the current sub-cluster
    readdump                Reads a cmmds directory dump from a file
                            (specified with -d/--dumpfile) and
                            o/p to stdout in a given format specified
                            using -f option.
options:
    -o/--owner=<uuid>:      Entry owner
    -u/--uuid=<uuid>:       Entry uuid
    -t/--type=<int>|<name>: Entry type
    -r/--rev=<int>:         Entry revision (-1 for latest)
    -i/--timeout=<int>:     Max time for wait (0 for infinite wait)
    -f/--format=<fmt>:      Output format (fmt should be one of
                            json/python/simple. Default is 'simple'
    -d/--dumpfile=<file>:   Filename to read the cmmds dump from.
    -p/--print-dump-hdr:    When CMMDS dump is read off the file, should
                            the dump file header be printed as well
    -v/--verbose=<int>:     Verbosity level
    -h/--help:              Print this help text
```

vdq

This command is another alternative to obtain a disk group composition and is much simpler in comparison to `esxcli`. In addition, we can also use this to obtain more information about the disks available to the VSAN cluster and if there are disks that cannot be added, it displays the reason as well. The `vdq -h` command displays the help menu. The two useful switches used with `vdq` are:

- `-q|--query`: This queries all the disks for eligibility for VSAN usage. It may be used with `--devices` to limit the query to only those devices.
- `-i|--info`: Dump out known VSAN disk mappings.

Consider the following example:

```
~ # vdq -Hq |less
DiskResults:
DiskResult[0]:
          Name:    naa.5000c5006bc03273
     VSANUUID:     52352867-2c80-e84b-c2ce-812a5c0a9b76
        State:     In-use for VSAN
       Reason:     None
IsSSD?:   0
IsPDL?:   0


DiskResult[2]:
          Name:    mpx.vmhba33:C0:T0:L0
     VSANUUID:
        State:     Ineligible for use by VSAN
       Reason:     Has partitions
IsSSD?:   0
IsPDL?:   0
```

Commands with longer output can be piped with `less` (for example, `add | less`). This displays output that can be scrolled. Also, the H switch provides a human-read able display. In this example, we can see an abstract where one of the magnetic disks (`IsSSD` equal to 0) is in use by VSAN. We also see the NAA ID of the device and the VSAN UUID it belongs to. However, as this is in use by another device, it reports as **Ineligible for use by VSAN** due to the reason that it has partitions. This specific device is actually the boot device on which ESXi is installed and understandably has the ESXi boot-related partitions. The PDL flag is related to permanent device loss; this is one of the intelligence behind VSAN on remedial action for a failed disk.

The `vdq -i` command displays the disk group composition:

```
~ # vdq -iH
Mappings:
DiskMapping[0]:
            SSD:   naa.5001e820026cfa60
             MD:   naa.5000c5006bc03273
             MD:   naa.5000c5006bc133d7


DiskMapping[2]:
            SSD:   naa.5001e820026cfa08
             MD:   naa.5000c5006bc22e17
             MD:   naa.5000c5006bc235b3
```

Ruby vSphere Console

Ruby vSphere Console (**RVC**) provides a holistic approach for troubleshooting VSAN. We will discuss some useful and exclusive command-line options available with RVC, while omitting some namespaces that provide the redundant output that is already covered with ESXCLI in the previous sections. RVC is bundled with vCenter Server 5.5 update 1 an upwards in both Windows-based vCenter and the vCenter appliance.

To access RVC from VCVA, you can simply key in the command `rvc` and point it to the local host or a remote vCenter that hosts the VSAN cluster.

From a Windows-based vCenter, you can launch RVC by following the outlined steps:

1. Log in to the Windows-based vCenter server.
2. Browse to C:\Program Files\VMware\Infrastructure\VirtualCenter Server\support\rvc.
3. Launch rvc.bat.
4. Key in the user credentials to get started.

To avoid performance issues and other complications, instead of using the production vCenter instance, you can choose to deploy another instance of the vCenter server appliance that may be used specifically for troubleshooting and performance monitoring purposes.

Manoeuvring around RVC

All of the outlined commands and output are from executing `rvc` from the vCenter server appliance that also manages the VSAN cluster. However, it can be used to access a remote vCenter that is hosting VSAN as well. The screenshot outlined here illustrates a connection to the local vCenter server:

```
localhost:~ # rvc
Host to connect to (user@host): root@10.112.102.202
password:
Welcome to RVC. Try the 'help' command.
0 /
1 10.112.102.202/
>
```

The filesystem structure and traversal is very similar to the UNIX filesystems, commencing at root (/). One can move from a vCenter object down to the data center and to specific VMs. The levels of the hierarchy and the equivalent vCenter object are outlined here:

Levels	RVC Object	vCenter Equivalent
1	/	Root
2	IP address	The vCenter server IP address
3	Data center	Data center object
3.1	Computers	Container of cluster
3.2	Networks	Port groups
3.3	Datastores	VMFS datastores
3.4	VMS	Virtual machines

For example, in order to execute a command at the cluster level, you can either change directory to the cluster and execute the command or supply the absolute or relative path to the cluster.

To get help with the commands and namespaces, you can invoke help as depicted here:

* `help namespace_name`
* `help namespace_name.command_name`

Consider the following example:

```
> help vsan
Commands:
enable_vsan_on_cluster: Enable VSAN on a cluster
disable_vsan_on_cluster: Disable VSAN on a cluster
host_consume_disks: Consumes all eligible disks on a host
host_info: Print VSAN info about a host
cluster_info: Print VSAN info about a cluster
disks_info: Print physical disk info about a host
cluster_set_default_policy: Set default policy on a cluster
object_info: Fetch information about a VSAN object
disk_object_info: Fetch information about all VSAN objects on a given
physical disk
cmmds_find: CMMDS Find
vm_object_info: Fetch VSAN object information about a VM
disks_stats: Show stats on all disks in VSAN
observer: Run observer
resync_dashboard: Resyncing dashboard
vm_perf_stats: VM perf stats
enter_maintenance_mode: Put hosts into maintenance mode


localhost:~ # rvc root@10.112.102.202
password:
0 /
1 10.112.102.202/
>
```

The IP address or hostname of the vCenter becomes the first directory under root (/).

Now, change the current directory to the vCenter object and run `ls` to list the subdirectory, list the equivalent objects under vCenter. Much of the file traversal is similar to the UNIX file structure:

```
>cd 10.112.102.202/
/10.112.102.202> ls
0 VSAN DC-BNG (datacenter)
/10.112.102.202>
```

Let's start by retrieving some information about the cluster. Prior to executing the command, you will need to change directory into the container of the specific object, that is, for retrieving information about VSAN Information. We know that VSAN is defined at the cluster level, so we can browse to the object as follows:

```
/10.112.102.202/VSAN DC-BNG> ls

0 storage/

1 computers [host]/

2 networks [network]/

3 datastores [datastore]/

4 vms [vm]/


/10.112.102.202/VSAN DC-BNG> cd 1


/10.112.102.202/VSAN DC-BNG/computers> ls

0 VSAN-Cluster (cluster): cpu 64 GHz, memory 154 GB


/10.112.102.202/VSAN DC-BNG/computers> cd 0


/10.112.102.202/VSAN DC-BNG/computers/VSAN-Cluster>ls

0 hosts/

1 resourcePool [Resources]: cpu 64.78/64.78/normal, mem 154.78/154.78/
normal


/10.112.102.202/VSAN DC-BNG/computers/VSAN DC-BNG> cd 0


/10.112.102.202/VSAN DC-BNG/computers/VSAN-Cluster/hosts> ls

0 10.109.10.107 (host): cpu 2*12*2.10 GHz, memory 68.00 GB

1 10.109.10.108 (host): cpu 2*12*2.10 GHz, memory 68.00 GB

2 10.109.10.109 (host): cpu 2*12*2.10 GHz, memory 68.00 GB
```

Once the relevant object is reached, we execute the command as outlined here:

```
/10.112.102.202/VSAN DC-BNG/computers/VSAN DC-BNG/hosts>vsan.host_info 0

VSAN enabled: yes

Cluster info:

  Cluster role: agent

  Cluster UUID: 526a4992-690a-4ca5-3bc9-6c7f056d7fd1
```

```
    Node UUID: 536a5c03-8268-4a67-a3ef-b8ca3af6a80e

    Member UUIDs: ["536a162d-2ab1-116e-d910-74867aee01ca", "536a20d1-60d3-
    ab9d-3206-74867aee0146", "536a5c03-8268-4a67-a3ef-b8ca3af6a80e"]
Storage info:
    Auto claim: yes
    Disk Mappings:
        SSD: Local Pliant Disk (naa.5001e820026cfa60) - 372 GB
        MD: Local SEAGATE Disk (naa.5000c5006bc03273) - 279 GB
        MD: Local SEAGATE Disk (naa.5000c5006bc133d7) - 279 GB
        SSD: Local Pliant Disk (naa.5001e820026cfa08) - 372 GB
        MD: Local SEAGATE Disk (naa.5000c5006bc22e17) - 279 GB
        MD: Local SEAGATE Disk (naa.5000c5006bc235b3) - 279 GB
NetworkInfo:
    Adapter: vmk1 (10.109.14.107)
```

Command-line options with RVC

In this section, we'll discuss the command-line options and namespaces available with RVC. These have been segregated into multiple sections based on their functionality.

Enabling and disabling VSAN

The following commands are the UI equivalent for enabling and disabling VSAN at the cluster level.

The syntax for this is as follows:

- enable_vsan_on_cluster
- disable_vsan_on_cluster

Consider the following example:

```
/localhost/VSAN DC-BNG/computers>vsan.enable_vsan_on_cluster 0
ReconfigureComputeResource VSAN DC-BNG: success
 10.109.10.107: success
 10.109.10.108: success
 10.109.10.109: success
```

Disk-related commands

The following commands revolve around disk-related operations:

- `host_consume_disks`: This command instructs the host to claim any unclaimed and eligible disks available on the hosts. It's only useful if hosts are configured on the manual claim mode.

- `host_wipe_vsan_disks`: This command wipes all the VSAN disks on a host. It can perhaps be used as a quick means by which to decommission a VSAN host.

- `disks.info`: This command provides some insightful disk-related information, specifically for disks that are not in use by VSAN. It displays partition information as well.

Consider the following example:

```
localhost/VSAN DC-BNG>vsan.disks_info computers/VSAN\ DC-BNG/
hosts/10.109.10.107
```

The output will be as shown in the following screenshot:

```
Disks on host 10.109.10.107:
+-------------------------------------------------+-------+--------+----------------------------------------------------------------+
| DisplayName                                     | isSSD | Size   | State                                                          |
+-------------------------------------------------+-------+--------+----------------------------------------------------------------+
| Local SEAGATE Disk (naa.5000c5006bc03273)       | MD    | 279 GB | inUse                                                          |
+-------------------------------------------------+-------+--------+----------------------------------------------------------------+
| Local USB Direct-Access (mpx.vmhba33:C0:T0:L0)  | MD    | 0 GB   | ineligible (Existing partitions found on disk 'mpx.vmhba33:C0:T0:L0'.) |
|                                                 |       |        |                                                                |
|                                                 |       |        | Partition table:                                               |
|                                                 |       |        | 5: 0.24 GB, type = vfat                                        |
|                                                 |       |        | 6: 0.24 GB, type = vfat                                        |
|                                                 |       |        | 7: 0.11 GB, type = coredump                                   |
|                                                 |       |        | 8: 0.28 GB, type = vfat                                        |
|                                                 |       |        | 9: 2.50 GB, type = coredump                                   |
+-------------------------------------------------+-------+--------+----------------------------------------------------------------+
```

Viewing the virtual machine layout

Some important information pertaining to understanding the layout of a virtual machine is that we can provide the path to the virtual machine container, the objects of the virtual machine, and their location on the physical device and host by executing the `vsan.vm_object_info` command.

```
/10.112.102.202/VSAN DC-BNG/computers> vsan.vm_object_info VSAN-Cluster/hosts/10.109.10.109/vms/vsantest/

VM vsantest:
Namespace directory
DOM Object: 871d4555-1308-d4e7-ad23-74867aee0146 (owner: 10.109.10.109, policy: forceProvisioning = 0,
hostFailuresToTolerate = 1, spbmProfileId = 6b9edaff-112a-4412-99d1-df522fcd3878, proportionalCapacity = [0, 100],
spbmProfileGenerationNumber = 0, cacheReservation = 0, stripeWidth = 1)

Witness: 881d4555-dd30-e260-c3b7-74867aee0146 (state: ACTIVE (5), host: 10.109.10.108, md: naa.5000c5006babf8bf,
ssd: naa.5001e820026cfa5c, usage: 0.0 GB)

RAID_1
Component: 881d4555-d3fb-e060-3dbe-74867aee0146 (state: ACTIVE (5), host: 10.109.10.107, md:
naa.5000c5006bc133d7, ssd: naa.5001e820026cfa08, usage: 0.1 GB)
Component: 881d4555-3f60-df60-616b-74867aee0146 (state: ACTIVE (5), host: 10.109.10.109, md: naa.5000c5006bad0a1f,
ssd: naa.5001e820026cfc4c, usage: 0.1 GB)
Disk backing: [vsanDatastore (1)] 871d4555-1308-d4e7-ad23-74867aee0146/vsantest.vmdk
```

Viewing the physical disk layout

To view the physical device's details, such as the NAA identifier, capacity, health, and so on, the vsan.disks_stats command comes in handy:

```
/10.112.102.202/VSAN DC-BNG/computers> ls
0 VSAN-Cluster (cluster): cpu 64 GHz, memory 154 GB
/10.112.102.202/VSAN DC-BNG/computers> vsan.disks_stats 0
+---------------------+----------------+-------+------+-------------+------+----------+--------+
|                     |                |       | Num  | Capacity    |      |          | Status |
| DisplayName         | Host           | isSSD | Comp | Total       | Used | Reserved | Health |
+---------------------+----------------+-------+------+-------------+------+----------+--------+
| naa.5001e820026cfa08 | 10.109.10.107 | SSD   | 0    | 260.83 GB   | 0 %  | 0 %      | OK     |
| naa.5000c5006bc133d7 | 10.109.10.107 | MD    | 4    | 279.25 GB   | 22 % | 22 %     | OK     |
| naa.5000c5006bc22e17 | 10.109.10.107 | MD    | 2    | 279.25 GB   | 1 %  | 1 %      | OK     |
+---------------------+----------------+-------+------+-------------+------+----------+--------+
| naa.5001e820026cfa60 | 10.109.10.107 | SSD   | 0    | 260.83 GB   | 0 %  | 0 %      | OK     |
| naa.5000c5006bc235b3 | 10.109.10.107 | MD    | 10   | 279.25 GB   | 59 % | 58 %     | OK     |
| naa.5000c5006bc03273 | 10.109.10.107 | MD    | 15   | 279.25 GB   | 77 % | 76 %     | OK     |
+---------------------+----------------+-------+------+-------------+------+----------+--------+
| naa.5001e820026cf85c | 10.109.10.108 | SSD   | 0    | 260.83 GB   | 0 %  | 0 %      | OK     |
| naa.5000c5006bacfd03 | 10.109.10.108 | MD    | 9    | 279.25 GB   | 72 % | 71 %     | OK     |
| naa.5000c5006baa94ab | 10.109.10.108 | MD    | 11   | 279.25 GB   | 77 % | 77 %     | OK     |
+---------------------+----------------+-------+------+-------------+------+----------+--------+
| naa.5001e820026cfa5c | 10.109.10.108 | SSD   | 0    | 260.83 GB   | 0 %  | 0 %      | OK     |
| naa.5000c5006baa978b | 10.109.10.108 | MD    | 4    | 279.25 GB   | 12 % | 11 %     | OK     |
| naa.5000c5006babf8bf | 10.109.10.108 | MD    | 4    | 279.25 GB   | 3 %  | 3 %      | OK     |
+---------------------+----------------+-------+------+-------------+------+----------+--------+
| naa.5001e820026cfa80 | 10.109.10.109 | SSD   | 0    | 260.83 GB   | 0 %  | 0 %      | OK     |
| naa.5000c5006bad0b7b | 10.109.10.109 | MD    | 3    | 279.25 GB   | 4 %  | 4 %      | OK     |
| naa.5000c5006baa7acf | 10.109.10.109 | MD    | 2    | 279.25 GB   | 6 %  | 5 %      | OK     |
+---------------------+----------------+-------+------+-------------+------+----------+--------+
| naa.5001e820026cfc4c | 10.109.10.109 | SSD   | 0    | 260.83 GB   | 0 %  | 0 %      | OK     |
| naa.5000c5006bad0a1f | 10.109.10.109 | MD    | 11   | 279.25 GB   | 48 % | 47 %     | OK     |
| naa.5000c5006bacfc7f | 10.109.10.109 | MD    | 9    | 279.25 GB   | 73 % | 72 %     | OK     |
+---------------------+----------------+-------+------+-------------+------+----------+--------+
/10.112.102.202/VSAN DC-BNG/computers>
```

To further delve into the detailed information of the objects in a device, the `disk_object_info` command is used. The command is executed at the cluster-container level and a parameter is passed in the NAA identifier of the device:

```
/10.112.102.202/VSAN DC-BNG/computers> vsan.disk_object_info 0 naa.5000c5006baa7acf
Physical disk naa.5000c5006baa7acf (52b2351f-a839-cf95-113e-1319e7887068):

DOM Object: 02124355-b484-7e1a-9d59-b8ca3af6a80e (owner: 10.109.10.107, policy:
hostFailuresToTolerate = 2, forceProvisioning = 1, proportionalCapacity = 100)
Context: Part of VM vcsa-bng-6: Disk: [vsanDatastore (1)] f5114355-2b77-cd86-1ff6-
b8ca3af6a80e/vcsa-bng-6_9.vmdk
Component: 03124355-9020-836d-da73-b8ca3af6a80e (state: ACTIVE (5), host: 10.109.10.109,
md: **naa.5000c5006baa7acf**, ssd: naa.5001e820026cfa80, usage: 10.0 GB)

DOM Object: 03124355-a12b-5397-2ef3-b8ca3af6a80e (owner: 10.109.10.107, policy:
hostFailuresToTolerate = 2, forceProvisioning = 1, proportionalCapacity = 100)
Context: Part of VM vcsa-bng-6: Disk: [vsanDatastore (1)] f5114355-2b77-cd86-1ff6-
b8ca3af6a80e/vcsa-bng-6_10.vmdk
Component: 04124355-641c-0eeb-037f-b8ca3af6a80e (state: ACTIVE (5), host: 10.109.10.109,
md: **naa.5000c5006baa7acf**, ssd: naa.5001e820026cfa80, usage: 5.0 GB)

/10.112.102.202/VSAN DC-BNG/computers>
```

cmmds_find

The `cmmds_find` command provides useful information, with regards to the disk/object health and layout.

The `cmmds_find -t DISK_USAGE` command, when executed at the cluster level, quickly reveals the health state of all the disks in the VSAN cluster. This is, perhaps, one of the first things to check when troubleshooting any issues with VSAN:

```
/localhost/VSAN DC-BNG/computers> vsan.cmmds_find 0 -t DISK_USAGE
+---+------------+--------------------------------------+---------------+---------+------------------------------+
| # | Type       | UUID                                 | Owner         | Health  | Content                      |
+---+------------+--------------------------------------+---------------+---------+------------------------------+
| 1 | DISK_USAGE | 52fc4634-b985-d403-878b-2d6d951be3b1 | 10.109.10.108 | Healthy | {"capacityReserved"=>0,      |
|   |            |                                      |               |         | "iopsReserved"=>0,           |
|   |            |                                      |               |         | "throughPutReserved"=>0,     |
|   |            |                                      |               |         | "l2CacheReserved"=>0,        |
|   |            |                                      |               |         | "l1CacheReserved"=>0}        |
| 2 | DISK_USAGE | 52914cfe-8e78-3917-c2e1-13c33494769e | 10.109.10.108 | Healthy | {"capacityReserved"=>30073159680, |
|   |            |                                      |               |         | "iopsReserved"=>0,           |
|   |            |                                      |               |         | "throughPutReserved"=>0,     |
|   |            |                                      |               |         | "l2CacheReserved"=>0,        |
|   |            |                                      |               |         | "l1CacheReserved"=>0}        |
| 3 | DISK_USAGE | 52ec0ac8-3c8d-4819-c1d3-731262a78202 | 10.109.10.108 | Healthy | {"capacityReserved"=>0,      |
|   |            |                                      |               |         | "iopsReserved"=>0,           |
|   |            |                                      |               |         | "throughPutReserved"=>0,     |
|   |            |                                      |               |         | "l2CacheReserved"=>0,        |
|   |            |                                      |               |         | "l1CacheReserved"=>0}        |
```

The -u option provides the ability to have a closer introspection of a specific object. Here we choose the first object's UUID in display. However, when troubleshooting, you may be specifically interested in the logs and error messages depicting issues with a certain object, and assessing the health and anomalies of that specific object:

```
/localhost/VSAN DC-BNG/computers> vsan.cmmds_find 0 -u 52fc4634-b985-d403-878b-2d6d951be8b1
+---+---------------+----------------------------------------+---------------+--------+----------------------------------------+
| # | Type          | UUID                                   | Owner         | Health | Content                                |
+---+---------------+----------------------------------------+---------------+--------+----------------------------------------+
| 1 | DISK          | 52fc4634-b985-d403-878b-2d6d951be8b1   | 10.109.10.108 | Healthy| {"capacity"=>280058920960,             |
|   |               |                                        |               |        |  "iops"=>20000,                        |
|   |               |                                        |               |        |  "iopsWritePenalty"=>10000000,         |
|   |               |                                        |               |        |  "throughput"=>200000000,              |
|   |               |                                        |               |        |  "throughputWritePenalty"=>0,          |
|   |               |                                        |               |        |  "latency"=>3400000,                   |
|   |               |                                        |               |        |  "latencyDeviation"=>0,                |
|   |               |                                        |               |        |  "reliabilityBase"=>10,                |
|   |               |                                        |               |        |  "reliabilityExponent"=>15,            |
|   |               |                                        |               |        |  "mtbf"=>2000000,                      |
|   |               |                                        |               |        |  "l2CacheCapacity"=>0,                 |
|   |               |                                        |               |        |  "l1CacheCapacity"=>16777216,          |
|   |               |                                        |               |        |  "isSsd"=>1,                           |
|   |               |                                        |               |        |  "ssdUuid"=>"52fc4634-b985-d403-878b-2d6d951be8b1", |
|   |               |                                        |               |        |  "volumeName"=>"NA"}                   |
| 2 | HEALTH_STATUS | 52fc4634-b985-d403-878b-2d6d951be8b1   | 10.109.10.108 | Healthy| {"healthFlags"=>0, "timestamp"=>60211375952} |
| 3 | DISK_USAGE    | 52fc4634-b985-d403-878b-2d6d951be8b1   | 10.109.10.108 | Healthy| {"capacityReserved"=>0,                |
|   |               |                                        |               |        |  "iopsReserved"=>0,                    |
|   |               |                                        |               |        |  "throughPutReserved"=>0,              |
|   |               |                                        |               |        |  "l2CacheReserved"=>0,                 |
|   |               |                                        |               |        |  "l1CacheReserved"=>0}                 |
```

resync.dashboard

The resync.dashboard command comes into play more often than any other command. As the name implies, it ensures that the storage objects are synchronized and organized. This operation is invoked implicitly or explicitly and reorganizes data based more commonly on failures to host/disk/network, and the changes made to storage policies or maintenance-related activities. The resync occurs silently without any intrusion to the VM and executes at the cluster level providing a detailed insight of objects for which sync is in progress and the status of the operation in terms of the byte count.

The command can be executed as follows:

```
/localhost/VSAN DC-BNG/computers/VSAN-Cluster> vsan.resync_dashboard ./
2015-01-24 00:40:02 -0500: Querying all VMs on VSAN ...
2015-01-24 00:40:02 -0500: Querying all objects in the system ...
2015-01-24 00:40:02 -0500: Got all the info, computing table ...
+-----------+-----------------+--------------+
| VM/Object | Syncing objects | Bytes to sync |
+-----------+-----------------+--------------+
+-----------+-----------------+--------------+
| Total     | 0               | 0.00 GB      |
+-----------+-----------------+--------------+
```

VSAN Observer

Given that VSAN has a layer of disks and a relatively complex architecture, monitoring and optimizing performance can be rather cumbersome. **VSAN Observer (VSOB)** is a powerful utility for monitoring a VSAN infrastructure and provides specific metrics to isolate a problematic/degraded component and also metrics indicating areas that need attention and optimization. Data is refreshed at an interval of 60 seconds, by default, and the average of the duration is displayed. This can be modified when required depending on the nature of the issue.

VSOB can either be run on live data or replayed on collected statistical data.

Monitoring live statistics

Outlined here is the procedure to invoke an observer to monitor the VSAN vCenter instance, and connect to the RVC instance through a browser:

The procedure for this is as follows:

1. Connect to the vCenter Server through Ruby vSphere Console.

2. Execute the `vsan.observer<Path to the cluster> --run-webserver -force` command:

   ```
   /localhost/VSAN DC-BNG/computers>vsan.observer VSAN-Cluster --run-
   webserver --force

   [2015-01-24 01:35:56] INFO  WEBrick 1.3.1

   [2015-01-24 01:35:56] INFO  ruby 1.9.2 (2011-07-09) [x86_64-linux]

   [2015-01-24 01:35:56] WARN  TCPServer Error: Address already in
   use - bind(2)

   Press <Ctrl>+<C> to stop observing at any point ...

   2015-01-24 01:35:56 -0500: Collect one inventory snapshot

   [2015-01-24 01:35:56] INFO  WEBrick::HTTPServer#start:

   pid=26721 port=8010

   Query VM properties: 0.04 sec

   Query Stats on 10.109.10.109: 1.67 sec (on ESX: 0.48, json size:
   274KB)

   Query Stats on 10.109.10.107: 1.72 sec (on ESX: 0.35, json size:
   311KB)

   Query Stats on 10.109.10.108: 1.82 sec (on ESX: 0.41, json size:
   306KB)
   ```

3. Note down the process ID and the port number.

4. By default, the observer monitors statistics for 2 hours, but it can be forcefully stopped by pressing *Ctrl + C* in the SSH session, or killing the process ID captured in the previous step.

5. To view the statistics, use your browser and navigate to the RVC IP address and port number captured in the third step. In this example, it is `https://10.112.102.202:8010/`.

6. Now, provide the credentials to log in on the webpage.

 Note that RVC connection may be triggered from the vCenter server hosting VSAN or from a remote vCenter server deployed only for monitoring purposes; the latter option is recommended to reduce the monitoring overhead.

The webpage will look like this:

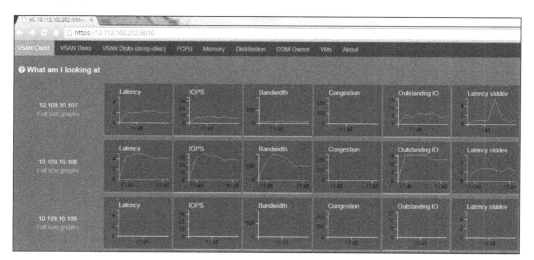

Offline diagnosis

An alternative to looking at live data is to redirect the output to a temporary location and replay the files. Note that content will be stored in the memory of the RVC/vCenter server, and will be redirected once the `vsan.observer` process is terminated.

The procedure of the diagnosis is as follows:

1. Execute the following command:

    ```
    /localhost/VSAN DC-BNG/computers>vsan.observer<path to
    cluster>VSAN-Cluster --generate-html-bundle /tmp
    ```

2. Now, terminate the collection by pressing *Ctrl + C* or kill the process:

    ```
    ^C2015-01-24 07:46:08 -0500: Execution interrupted, wrapping up
    ...

    2015-01-24 07:46:09 -0500: Done writing HTML bundle to /tmp/vsan-
    observer-2015-01-24.07-46-08.tar.gz
    ```

3. Note the filename and location. You can use WinSCP/SCP or similar tools to export the file to a client machine (any operating system with a browser).

4. Extract the `*tar.gz` file from your client machine.

5. Open the `stats.html` file in you browser, as follows:

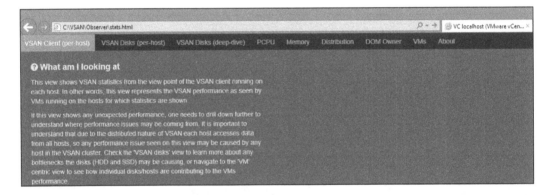

Interpreting VSOB data and key metrics

As with any disk performance-related issue, there are very generic metrics that can provide a directive to troubleshoot the issue. VSOB provides some additional metrics to verify and validate whether the issues are specific to VSAN-related components.

VSOB follows a basic color code to flag unhealthy metrics associated with a component with a red underline, green for healthy metrics, and grey for information not yet available.

The typical workflow is to narrow down components contribute to the red flag. Let's take a closer look at the metrics available:

- **Latency**: This is the time taken to complete an I/O. A lower value implies better performance, but there is no definitive reference value to quantify good or bad performance, and this is subject to the quality of the disk used. VSOB uses specific threshold values as an upper limit.

- **IOPS**: This is the number of I/O per second that is being utilized by the workloads. The amount of IOPS should be within the permissible threshold of what each of the SSDs can handle. If there are evictions, the IOPS capability of the magnetic disks come into play.

- **Congestion**: Congestion is a sign of a bottleneck in the I/O path, I/O travels from the virtual machine down to the disks, and if there any intermediate layers that cannot sustain the rate of inflow, then there is a natural increase in latency. This mostly happens when moving the data from the SSD to magnetic disks. If we do not see any congestion, it is safe to presume that the SSD is efficiently servicing all or most of the I/O.

- **Read cache hit rate**: This metric indicates whether the flash disk is able to service the reads or has to reference the read to the magnetic disk. In general, the read cache is the active dataset of the workloads on the SSD. A lower read cache hit rate indicates that the read has overflown to the magnetic disk, which is an indication to revisit if the SSD has sufficient space to accommodate all the workloads' reads.

- **Evictions**: This metric is indicative of data being offloaded to a magnetic disk to facilitate newer write content on the SSD. Depending on the inbound I/O to the SSD, there can be a slowdown in the performance when evictions are observed. Similar to the read cache hit rate, this metric is indicative of the need to revisit the SSD sizing.

- **Write buffer fill**: This metric is similar to evictions, but is more proactive. It indicates the utilization of the write buffer size used on the SSD.

- **Outstanding I/O**: These are the inflight I/O that have been shot off by workloads and are pending completion depending on whether the I/O is being serviced by a local SSD, remote SSD, local magnetic disk, or remote magnetic disk. This metric is important to measure performance. Lesser I/O implies faster performance.

- **Latency standard deviation**: Latency is being monitored over a period of time and the amount of fluctuation is denoted by this metric. Higher deviation implies that there has been fluctuation in the latency. In general, this could be due to a sudden burst in IOPS or anomalies with one or more disks.

While we have looked at some of the key metrics here, you can get more detailed insight and additional metrics that are available in full-size graph to access the full-sized graph. You can click on the hyperlink adjacent to the hostname or IP address, as illustrated in the following screenshot:

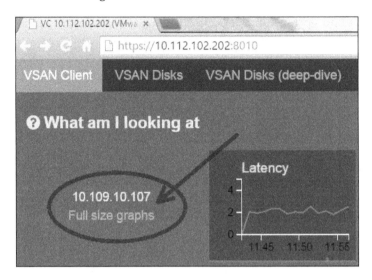

Here is an example of a full-size graph:

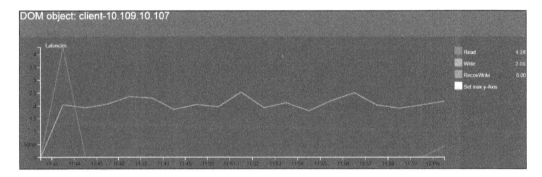

Summary

VMware has empowered administrators to be self-sufficient in administrating VSAN with an array of troubleshooting and monitoring utilities. Furthermore, the utilities have been very intuitive; some of which are UI-based and user friendly.

Some of these utilities were previously kept only for internal consumption and eventually made it to the public domain. On similar lines, for experimental use, there are more such tools available at `https://labs.vmware.com/flings`; these cut across multiple product lines.

In the next chapter, we will review the newer features and improvements to the existing ones, scalability enhancements, and architectural changes with in the latest generation of VSAN.

What's New in VSAN 6.0?

So far, we have looked exhaustively at the crux of VSAN through its first generation. In this chapter, we will discuss the new features, enhancements, and architectural changes done to VMware Virtual SAN in the latest version, VSAN 6.0, that is embedded with vSphere 6.x.

To avoid any ambiguity about the versions and generations that will be interchangeably used, the first generation of VSAN (VSAN 1.0) is embedded with VMware ESXi 5.5 U1 and U2, and managed by VMware vCenter Server 5.5 U1 or U2.

The second generation of VSAN (VSAN 2.0), is embedded with VMware ESXi 6.0 and managed by VMware vCenter 6.0.

In this chapter, we will discuss:

- Architectural changes
- Feature enhancements
- Serviceability improvements
- Scalability enhancements

VSAN architecture types

The support for all-flash VSAN is perhaps the most significant enhancement on the previous generation of VSAN. This implies that we now have the following two types of disk group compositions for Virtual SAN:

- Hybrid VSAN
- All-flash VSAN

The VMware compatibility matrix has a field added to include whether the specific I/O controllers support the all-flash mode or the hybrid mode, or both.

Similarly, SSD devices include support explicitly if the device is suited and certified for the all-flash caching tier, the all-flash capacity tier, and the hybrid caching tier.

The following two screenshots reflect this change in the VMware compatibility list available at http://www.vmware.com/resources/compatibility/search. php?deviceCategory=vsan:

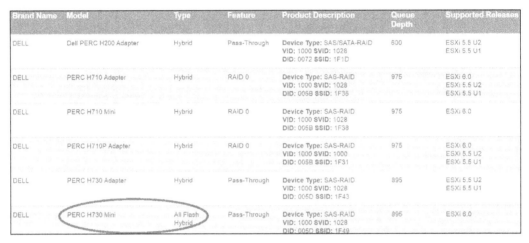

Brand Name	Model	Type	Feature	Product Description	Queue Depth	Supported Releases
DELL	Dell PERC H200 Adapter	Hybrid	Pass-Through	Device Type: SAS/SATA-RAID VID: 1000 SVID: 1028 DID: 0072 SSID: 1F1D	600	ESXi 5.5 U2 ESXi 5.5 U1
DELL	PERC H710 Adapter	Hybrid	RAID 0	Device Type: SAS-RAID VID: 1000 SVID: 1028 DID: 005B SSID: 1F35	975	ESXi 6.0 ESXi 5.5 U2 ESXi 5.5 U1
DELL	PERC H710 Mini	Hybrid	RAID 0	Device Type: SAS-RAID VID: 1000 SVID: 1028 DID: 005B SSID: 1F38	975	ESXi 6.0
DELL	PERC H710P Adapter	Hybrid	RAID 0	Device Type: SAS-RAID VID: 1000 SVID: 1000 DID: 005B SSID: 1F31	975	ESXi 6.0 ESXi 5.5 U2 ESXi 5.5 U1
DELL	PERC H730 Adapter	Hybrid	Pass-Through	Device Type: SAS-RAID VID: 1000 SVID: 1028 DID: 005D SSID: 1F43	895	ESXi 5.5 U2 ESXi 5.5 U1
DELL	PERC H730 Mini	All Flash Hybrid	Pass-Through	Device Type: SAS-RAID VID: 1000 SVID: 1028 DID: 005D SSID: 1F49	895	ESXi 6.0

I/O controller compatibility

In the following screenshot, we can observe an example of SSD suited for VSAN all-flash caching, as well as VSAN hybrid caching:

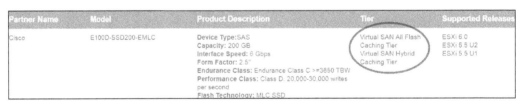

Partner Name	Model	Product Description	Tier	Supported Releases
Cisco	E100D-SSD200-EMLC	Device Type:SAS Capacity: 200 GB Interface Speed: 6 Gbps Form Factor: 2.5" Endurance Class: Endurance Class C >=3650 TBW Performance Class: Class D. 20,000-30,000 writes per second Flash Technology: MLC SSD	Virtual SAN All Flash Caching Tier Virtual SAN Hybrid Caching Tier	ESXi 6.0 ESXi 5.5 U2 ESXi 5.5 U1

SSD compatibility

In the following screenshot, we can observe an SSD device that can only be used for the all-flash capacity tier:

Partner Name	Model	Product Description	Tier	Supported Releases
DELL	400GB Solid State Drive SATA, Mix Use MLC 6Gbps 2.5in Hot-plug Drive	Device Type:SATA Capacity: 400 GB Interface Speed: 6 Gbps Form Factor: 2.5" Endurance Class: Endurance Class B >=1825 TBW Performance Class: Class C 10,000-20,000 writes per second Flash Technology: eMLC SSD	Virtual SAN All Flash Capacity Tier	ESXi 6.0

Hybrid VSAN

Disk groups that are formulated with the combination of magnetic disks and flash devices are termed as a hybrid VSAN. VMware ESXi and vCenter Server 5.5 update 1 and update 2 support only the hybrid architecture of VSAN. The earlier discussions in this book have delved deep into this type of disk group composition. With the advent of the new all-flash VSAN architecture, there is a need to distinguish it the traditional architecture; hence, we call it a hybrid VSAN.

All-flash VSAN

As the name implies, the all-flash VSAN enables a VSAN cluster to be entirely made up of flash devices. In essence, a disk group is made up of very fast and durable write cache SSDs that serve as the caching layer for the write I/O. The more cost-effective SSDs that are used provide the storage capacity for persistently storing the data. The SSD used for capacity will service read I/O directly. The writes that are first written to the caching tier SSD are eventually destaged as needed onto the lower cost capacity SSD. The thumb rule to size 10 percent for caching still holds good; the difference being the entire 10 percent of caching is reserved for writes and there is no read cache concept unlike hybrid.

The following figure describes the I/O flow in an all-flash setup:

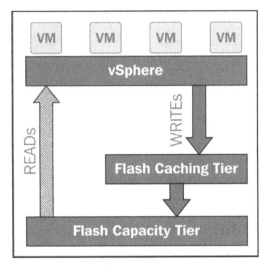

All-flash VSAN

Disk group creation for an all-flash setup

To leverage the all-flash VSAN, an administrator has to manually distinguish the SSD that will be used for caching from those that will be used for capacity. This is done by tagging the flash device that ought to be used for capacity.

Administrators can perform this step through the ESXCLI or RVC namespaces.

Tagging flash capacity devices through ESXCLI

Execute the following ESXCLI namespace to identify the flash devices to be used for capacity and to tag them:

```
esxcli storage core device list
```

Note down the NAA identifier of the flash devices to be used for capacity, as follows:

```
esxcli vsan storage tag add -d <inject naa id from step 1> -t
capacityFlash
```

Tagging flash capacity devices through Ruby vSphere Client

The steps are very similar to ESXCLI, through the syntax; identify the flash device and tag it as `capacity_flash`.

Now, execute the following command:

```
vsan.host_claim_disks_differently --disk <naa.id> --claim-type capacity_
flash
```

Validation

To validate whether the changes are applied successfully to the appropriate flash devices, you can execute the following command from the ESXi host:

```
vdq -q -d <NAA ID>
```

The attribute that confirms that the flash device has been tagged successfully is `IsCapacityFlash`. This variable will be set to `1`. The output of the previous command will look something like this:

```
# vdq -q -d naa.5000c5006bc235b3
\{
"Name"              :   "naa.5000c5006bc235b3",
"VSANUUID          :   "",
"State"             :   "Eligible for use by VSAN",
"ChecksumSupport"   :   "0",
"Reason"            :   "None",
"IsSSD"             :   "1",
"IsCapacityFlash"   :   "1",
"IsPDL"             :   "0",
    \},
```

Once the flash devices are segregated by capacity tier, the automatic or manual disk claim processes can be triggered in a similar way to hybrid disk group creation.

Points to remember with all-flash VSAN

There are some key considerations and caveats to be kept in mind when adopting an all-flash architecture:

- All-flash is supported by VSAN 6.0 only

- The VSAN network needs to have a 10 GbE NIC

- There can be seven flash devices per disk group with a maximum of one device for caching

- A hybrid disk group should not be mixed with the all-flash disk group in a single VSAN cluster

- Cache sizing is recommended to be 10 percent of consumed space

- The entire cache device is reserved for the write I/O

- The maximum size used for caching is 600 GB per disk group, irrespective of the total capacity of the flash device, a maximum of 600 GB will be used

- If additional caching space is required, the disk group should be created accordingly

The new on-disk format

The first generation of VSAN used the VMFS-L (v1) filesystem, which is a modified version of VMFS. With the second generation of VSAN, there is a new on-disk format called **VSAN File System** (**VSANFS**). This new filesystem significantly enhances snapshot scalability and clone management support. VSAN 6.0 supports both the v1 and v2 filesystem types. However, to uncover the newer features and enhancements, the filesystem from a vSphere 5.5 deployment needs to be upgraded.

If the cluster is created from scratch on vSphere 6.0, the new filesystem is automatically used.

Snapshot enhancements

As an outcome of leveraging the new on-disk format, snapshot handling at a filesystem level has been modified. The new snapshot format with VSAN 6.0 is vsanSparse. This effectively replaces vmfsSparse, which has certain basic limitations in terms of performance and scalability. While there are no user-visible manifestations of vsanSparse, administrators can be assured that there is a relative performance improvement over the previous version.

The fault domain

While VMware HA was initially introduced, one key aspect when designing the HA cluster layout was to ensure that hosts are distributed across racks/chassis to avoid a single point of failure in terms of racks or chassis. This implementation has trickled up into the VSAN layer. In its first generation, objects were distributed across hosts in a cluster and the number of failures to tolerate ensured that the host failures could be sustained. However, this did not factor into account whether the hosts were part of the same rack or another rack. Hence, there could have been a situation wherein all the hosts holding the object may end up being on one single rack. VSAN 6.0 introduces an enhancement with fault domains that have rack awareness. This effectively mitigates a single point of failure at the rack level.

In the following figure, we see a three-node cluster stacked in the same rack and connected to the same top of the rack switch and power outlet. This entire stack can be thought of as one fault domain — a single point of failure. The object is to move the hosts to alternate racks and define each rack as a fault domain:

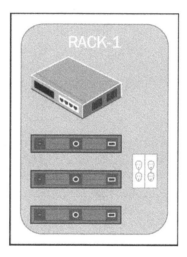

Let's discuss this with the help of an example. A virtual machine with FTT (n) set to 1 requires $2n+1$ number of hosts; three hosts to sustain failures if the fault domain is enabled in the cluster. The VSAN logic will ensure that the objects are distributed on hosts across multiple fault domains, even if there are multiple hosts available on a single fault domain. The following image demonstrates server distribution across racks and the fault domain definition.

Ideally, the effectiveness of the fault domain feature is dependent on ensuring that a similar layout is physically implemented in the data center.

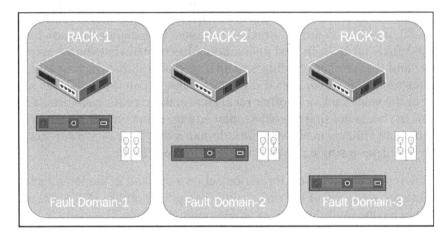

In a similar fashion, with the increasing values of FTT, the number of fault domains should increase as per the *2n+1* rule. In short, the failures of all hosts under a single fault domain is considered to be a single failure, similar to one host failure in the context of FTT.

JBOD support

While VSAN continues to increase the scalability, there are hardware limitations with the amount of storage that can be added to server hardware, this specifically holds good with servers, that has very less or no local storage. VSAN 6.0 supports **Just a Bunch Of Disks (JBODs)**. This implies that servers can have externally attached drive enclosures that can participate and contribute storage to a VSAN cluster.

Serviceability improvements

There are a few usability or serviceability improvements with VSAN 6.0 as well. These help in the overall improvement in the administration of VSAN.

LED locators

For troubleshooting purposes, VSAN 6.0 now includes the ability to enable or disable LEDs through the vSphere web client. This helps to locate a failed device.

The procedure to enable or disable the locator LEDs for a specific device is outlined here:

1. Browse to the VSAN cluster through the vSphere web client navigator.
2. Navigate to **Manage | Settings**.
3. Navigate to **Disk Management**.
4. Select the host to view the list of devices.
5. Select the devices and enable or disable the locator LED.

A what-if scenario

An additional field is included in the project the capacity usage of each VMDK on the VSAN datastore. This provides a fair estimation to the administrator of the current usage or projected usage with changes to the storage policy.

The rebalance operation

VSAN constantly monitors the capacity threshold of all the devices on the capacity tier. If the used capacity of a magnetic disk is above 80 percent, a rebalance operation gets automatically triggered that tries to redistribute data to bring the used capacity below 80 percent. In general, you observe that the capacity gets imbalanced when there is a device failure or if there is a maintenance-related operation (data migration or evacuation) on any of the nodes. The rebalance operation will eventually redistribute capacity across the magnetic disks.

The rebalance process can also be triggered manually through RVC:

1. Check the current distribution by executing the following command:

    ```
    vsan.check_limits /localhost/VSAN\ DC-BNG/computers/VSAN-Cluster/
    ```

```
> vsan.check_limits /localhost/VSAN\ DC-BNG/computers/VSAN-Cluster/
2015-04-01 15:20:35 +0000: Gathering stats from all hosts ...
2015-04-01 15:20:37 +0000: Gathering disks info ...
2015-04-01 15:20:37 +0000: Fetching VSAN disk info from 10.109.10.107 (may take a moment) ...
2015-04-01 15:20:37 +0000: Fetching VSAN disk info from 10.109.10.108 (may take a moment) ...
2015-04-01 15:20:37 +0000: Fetching VSAN disk info from 10.109.10.109 (may take a moment) ...
2015-04-01 15:20:42 +0000: Done fetching VSAN disk infos
+-----------------+--------------------+---------------------------+
| Host            | RDT                | Disks                     |
+-----------------+--------------------+---------------------------+
| 10.109.10.107   | Assocs: 104/20000  | Components: 25/3000        |
|                 | Sockets: 40/10000  | naa.5000c5006bc133d7: 0%  |
|                 | Clients: 14        | naa.5000c5006bc22e17: 0%  |
|                 | Owners: 16         | naa.5000c5006bc235b3: 59% |
|                 |                    | naa.5000c5006bc03273: 76% |
|                 |                    | naa.5001e820026cfa60: 0%  |
|                 |                    | naa.5001e820026cfa08: 0%  |
| 10.109.10.108   | Assocs: 49/20000   | Components: 22/3000        |
|                 | Sockets: 33/10000  | naa.5000c5006baa978b: 0%  |
|                 | Clients: 5         | naa.5000c5006bacfd03: 71% |
|                 | Owners: 4          | naa.5001e820026cf85c: 0%  |
|                 |                    | naa.5001e820026cfa5c: 0%  |
|                 |                    | naa.5000c5006babf8bf: 0%  |
|                 |                    | naa.5000c5006baa94ab: 76% |
| 10.109.10.109   | Assocs: 23/20000   | Components: 20/3000        |
|                 | Sockets: 23/10000  | naa.5000c5006bad0b7b: 0%  |
|                 | Clients: 0         | naa.5001e820026cfa80: 0%  |
|                 | Owners: 1          | naa.5000c5006bacfc7f: 73% |
|                 |                    | naa.5000c5006bad0a1f: 48% |
|                 |                    | naa.5001e820026cfc4c: 0%  |
|                 |                    | naa.5000c5006baa7acf: 0%  |
+-----------------+--------------------+---------------------------+
```

2. Execute a rebalance by running the following command:

    ```
    vsan.proactive_rebalance [opts]<Path to ClusterComputeResource>
    --start
    ```

Scalability

VSAN 6.0 specifically debunked the scalability myths perceived earlier and has evolved from 8 nodes to 32 nodes. With the current release, it can scale up to 64 nodes in a cluster and can host 6400 virtual machines per cluster. The components per VSAN host has increased from 3000 to 9000. More specific details and updated information is available online in the VMware portal at https://www.vmware.com/pdf/vsphere6/r60/vsphere-60-configuration-maximums.pdf.

Scalability metrics	Virtual SAN 5.5	Virtual SAN 6.0 Hybrid	Virtual SAN 6.0 All-flash
Hosts per cluster	32	64	64
VMs per host	100	200	200
IOPS per host	20000	40000	90000

Summary

In this chapter, we closely evaluated the key differences between VSAN 6.0 and its predecessor. While some of the enhancements discussed here are open to administrators, there are several enhancements behind the scenes. The all-flash supportability kicks up a few notches with higher IOPS capability and, more importantly, more uniform and reduced latency for the workloads. The filesystem cutover to the newer VSAN filesystem (v2) opens the door for several enhancements on the cloning and snapshot capabilities and also mitigates the conventional limitations that exists even today on regular VMFS volumes.

The first generation of VSAN went GA on March 11, 2014 through vSphere 5.5 update 1 and, within a year, VMware marched ahead with the second generation—VSAN 6.0. The numerous enhancements and architectural changes reflect how disruptively the product is emerging in the field.

The signs look clear, the future of software-defined storage is being defined and redefined with VSAN leading the revolution.

Index

A

all-flash VSAN
  about 125
  considerations 128
  disk group, creating 126
architecture types, VSAN 6.0
  about 123, 124
  all-flash VSAN 125
  hybrid VSAN 125

B

building blocks, VSAN
  about 13
  disk groups 14
  Storage Policy Based
     Management (SPBM) 14
  VMFS-Local (VMFS-L) 14

C

cache-to-capacity ratio
  about 83
  availability 85
  capacity 84
  performance 84
capacity planning
  about 23
  guidelines 23
  VSAN sizing utility 26-28
  workloads, profiling 24, 25
cluster, ESXCLI namespace 101, 102
cluster level object manager (CLOM) 70
**cluster monitoring, membership, and
    directory services (CMMDS) 69**

command-line options, RVC
  about 111
  disk-related commands 112
  physical disk layout, viewing 113, 114
  virtual machine layout, viewing 112
  VSAN, disabling 111
  VSAN, enabling 111
components 63, 67

D

datastore, ESXCLI namespace
  about 94, 95
  get command 95
  set command 95
disk boot device
  boot from SAN 16
  local storage 16
  SD 16
  USB 16
Diskful Writes Per Day (DWPD) 18
disk group
  about 33, 34, 126
  capacity devices, tagging through
     ESXCL 126
  capacity devices, tagging through Ruby
     vSphere Client 127
  creating, for all-flash VSAN
  validation 127
disk-related commands
  disks.info 112
  host_consume_disks 112
  host_wipe_vsan_disks 112
distributed object manager (DOM)
  about 70
  local log structured object manager
     (LSOM) 70, 71

Distributed Virtual Switch (DVS) 42
dots
  between components and witnesses,
    connecting 68
  between policies and objects,
    connecting 67, 68

E

ESXCLI namespace
  about 93, 94, 104
  cluster 94, 101, 102
  cmmds-tool command 105
  datastore 94, 95
  esxcli vsan maintenancemode 104
  esxcli vsan trace 104, 105
  get command 102
  join command 102
  leave command 102
  maintenancemode 94
  network 94-96
  policy 94, 103, 104
  restore command 102
  RVC 107
  storage 94, 97, 99, 100
  trace 94
  URL 101
  vdq command 106
EVO: RAIL
  about 20, 30
  VMware guidelines 31

F

Failures to Tolerate (FTT) 66
fault domain 129, 130

H

hardware specifications, VSAN cluster 36
high availability (HA)
  and VSAN 71, 72
  flash device failure 73
  host failure 74
  magnetic disk failure 72, 73
hybrid VSAN 125
Hyper-Converged Infrastructure
  Appliance (HCIA) 20

I

influencing factors, workloads
  consolidation ratio 25
  IOPS ratio 25
  SSD to HDD ratio 25
Input/Output Operations Per Second
  (IOPS) 58
installation workflow, VSAN cluster
  about 35
  Phase I 36
  Phase II 36
  Phase III 36
  Phase IV 36
  Phase V 36
internal building blocks, VSAN
  about 68
  cluster level object manager (CLOM) 70
  cluster monitoring, membership, and
    directory services (CMMDS) 69
  distributed object manager (DOM) 70
  reliable datagram transport (RDT) 69
I/O anatomy
  about 59
  data, destaging to magnetic disk 60
  read cache 61
  write buffer 59

J

jumbo frame
  about 76
  enabling, on vNetwork Distributed
    vSwitch (vDS) 76
  URL 76
Just a Bunch Of Disks (JBODs) support 130

L

local log structured object manager
  (LSOM) 70

M

magnetic disks
  about 83
  cache-to-capacity ratio 83
  I/O controllers 83

metrics, VSOB
  congestion 119
  evictions 119
  IOPS 119
  latency 119
  latency standard deviation 119
  outstanding I/O 119
  read cache hit rate 119
  write buffer fill 119
multicast traffic, VSAN 34

N

Network Attached Storage (NAS) 3
network, ESXCLI namespace
  about 95
  clear command 96
  list command 96
  remove command 96
  restore command 96
Network Interface Cards (NICs) 29
Network IO control (NIOC)
  about 78
  isolation 78-81
  limits 78-81
  Quality of Service (QoS) 81, 82
  shares 78-81
network optimizations
  about 75, 76
  jumbo frame 76
  network interface speed 77
  Network IO control (NIOC) 78
  parameters 76
number of failures to tolerate capability
  about 51
  scenario based examples 51-53

O

object
  about 63
  snapshot delta-disks 66
  swap object 64
  virtual disks 66
  virtual machine home namespace 65, 66
on-disk format
  about 128
  snapshot enhancements 128

P

physical disk layout, viewing
  cmmds_find command, using 114, 115
  resync.dashboard, using 115
policies
  need for 46
  SPBM 46
  VSAN datastore, capabilities 48
policy, ESXCLI namespace
  about 103, 104
  cleardefault command 103
  getdefault command 103
  setdefault command 103

Q

Quality of Service (QoS) 81, 82

R

read cache, I/O
  workflow 61, 62
reliable datagram transport (RDT) 69
Ruby vSphere Console (RVC)
  about 107
  command-line options, using 111
  manoeuvring around 108, 109

S

scalability, VSAN 6.0
  about 132, 133
  URL 132
scale-out design 86
SDDC
  about 1-3
  Computing/server virtualization 3
  pillars 3
  Software-Defined Networking 3
  Software-Defined Storage 3
serviceability improvements, VSAN 6.0
  about 130
  LED locators 131
  rebalance operation 131, 132
  what-if scenario 131
shapes and sizes, VSAN
  Custom built 28, 29

EVO: RAIL 28, 30
VSAN ready nodes 28-30
software components, VSAN
about 93
cluster monitoring 93
directory services 93
distributed object manager 93
log structured object manager 93
membership 93
Software-defined Data Center. *See* **SDDC**
Software-Defined Storage
about 3, 4
hyper-converged solutions 5, 6
storage, choices 4
storage, software-based 5
storage, traditional 4
solid state disk (SSD) 10
storage area network (SAN) 3
Storage Based Policy Based
Management (SPBM)
about 46
VSAN storage providers, managing 56
vSphere APIs for Storage Awareness
(VASA) 55
working 55
storage configuration optimizations
about 82
magnetic disks 83
storage, ESXCLI namespace
about 97, 99, 100
add command 97
list command 97
remove command 97
Storage Policy Based Management
(SPBM) 14

V

VDP
local backup, creating through 87, 88
local backup to VMFS/NFS, creating
through 88
remote backup, creating through 88
Virtual Machine File System (VMFS) 14
Virtual SAN. *See* **VSAN**
VMFS-Local (VMFS-L) 14
VMware Compatibility Guide (VCG) 82

VMware compatibility list
URL 124
VMware KB
URL 42, 76, 81
VMWare Standard vSwitch (VSS) 42
VMware Virtual SAN 6-8
VMware vSphere documentation
URL 38
vNetwork Distributed vSwitch (vDS) 76
VSAN
about 10-12
advantages 9, 10
and high availability (HA) 71, 72
architecture 57, 58
building blocks 13
disk boot device 16
disk controller 17
disk flash devices 18
EVO: RAIL 20
features 10
internal building blocks 68
Key concepts 34
magnetic disks 19
network requirements 19
options 20
protecting, with vSphere Replication
(VR) 89, 90
ready nodes 20
ready nodes, URL 85
shapes and sizes 28
sizing tool, URL 82
software components 93
software requirements 15
starting with 15
storage traffic 34
URL 18
VSAN 6.0
about 123
architecture types 123
fault domain 129
Just a Bunch Of Disks (JBODs) 130
on-disk format 128
scalability 132
serviceability improvements 130
VSAN cluster
disk groups 33
hardware specifications 36

installation workflow 35
key concepts 33
layout 37
network layout 38
prerequisite checklist 35
server node 37
setting up 38-42
VSAN network 34
VSAN datastore, capabilities
about 48
accessing 49, 50
flash read cache reservation 53, 54
force provisioning 54
number of disk stripes per object 50
number of failures to tolerate 51
object space reservation 55
VSAN File System (VSANFS) 128
VSAN network
multicast traffic 34
storage traffic 34
VSAN Observer (VSOB)
about 116
data, interpreting 118
key metrics, interpreting 119, 120
live statistics, monitoring 116, 117
offline diagnosis 118
VSAN ready nodes
installation 43
VSAN sizing utility
about 26, 27
URL 26
VSAN workloads
backing up 87
local backup, creating through VDP 87, 88
local backup VMFS/NFS, creating through
    VDP 88
remote backup, creating through VDP 88
vSphere Replication (VR) 89, 90
vSphere Data Protection (VDP) 87
vSphere installation bundles (VIBs) 36
vStorage APIs for Storage Awareness
    (VASA) 47

W

witness 63, 67
workflow, troubleshooting
configuration limit, validating 92
hardware validating 92
workloads
classifying 24
influencing factors 25
profiles, URL 25
profiling 24

Thank you for buying
Getting Started with VMware Virtual SAN

About Packt Publishing

Packt, pronounced 'packed', published its first book, *Mastering phpMyAdmin for Effective MySQL Management*, in April 2004, and subsequently continued to specialize in publishing highly focused books on specific technologies and solutions.

Our books and publications share the experiences of your fellow IT professionals in adapting and customizing today's systems, applications, and frameworks. Our solution-based books give you the knowledge and power to customize the software and technologies you're using to get the job done. Packt books are more specific and less general than the IT books you have seen in the past. Our unique business model allows us to bring you more focused information, giving you more of what you need to know, and less of what you don't.

Packt is a modern yet unique publishing company that focuses on producing quality, cutting-edge books for communities of developers, administrators, and newbies alike. For more information, please visit our website at www.packtpub.com.

About Packt Enterprise

In 2010, Packt launched two new brands, Packt Enterprise and Packt Open Source, in order to continue its focus on specialization. This book is part of the Packt Enterprise brand, home to books published on enterprise software – software created by major vendors, including (but not limited to) IBM, Microsoft, and Oracle, often for use in other corporations. Its titles will offer information relevant to a range of users of this software, including administrators, developers, architects, and end users.

Writing for Packt

We welcome all inquiries from people who are interested in authoring. Book proposals should be sent to author@packtpub.com. If your book idea is still at an early stage and you would like to discuss it first before writing a formal book proposal, then please contact us; one of our commissioning editors will get in touch with you.

We're not just looking for published authors; if you have strong technical skills but no writing experience, our experienced editors can help you develop a writing career, or simply get some additional reward for your expertise.

VMware vSphere 5.5 Cookbook

ISBN: 978-1-78217-285-7   Paperback: 560 pages

A task-oriented guide with over 150 practical recipes to install, configure, and manage VMware vSphere components

1. Explore the use of command line interface (CLI) to consistently configure the environment and automate it reasonably.

2. Discover the best practices to deploy stateless and statefull ESXi hosts and upgrade them.

3. Simplified and to-the-point theory to manage vSphere Storage and Networking Environment.

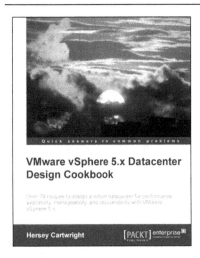

VMware vSphere 5.x Datacenter Design Cookbook

ISBN: 978-1-78217-700-5   Paperback: 260 pages

Over 70 recipes to design a virtual datacenter for performance, availability manageability, and recoverability with VMware vSphere 5.x

1. Innovative recipes, offering numerous practical solutions when designing virtualized datacenters.

2. Identify the design factors—requirements, assumptions, constraints, and risks—by conducting stakeholder interviews and performing technical assessments.

3. Increase and guarantee performance, availability, and workload efficiency with practical steps and design considerations.

Please check **www.PacktPub.com** for information on our titles

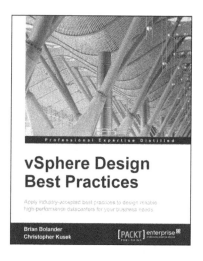

vSphere Design Best Practices

ISBN: 978-1-78217-626-8   Paperback: 126 pages

Apply industry-accepted best practices to design reliable high-performance datacenters for your business needs

1. Learn how to utilize the robust features of VMware to design, architect, and operate a virtual infrastructure using the VMware vSphere platform.

2. Customize your vSphere Infrastructure to fit your business needs with specific use-cases for live production environments.

3. Explore the vast opportunities available to fully leverage your virtualization infrastructure.

Troubleshooting vSphere Storage

ISBN: 978-1-78217-206-2   Paperback: 150 pages

Become a master at troubleshooting and solving common storage issues in your vSphere environment

1. Identify key issues that affect vSphere storage visibility, performance, and capacity.

2. Comprehend the storage metrics and statistics that are collected in vSphere.

3. Get acquainted with the many vSphere features that can proactively protect your environment.

Please check **www.PacktPub.com** for information on our titles